RESCRIPT

Daily Gratitude Journal

Dr. Colleen Georges

Copyright © 2023 Colleen Georges, Ed.D.
All rights reserved.

Printed in the United States of America
Published by RESCRIPT Your Story LLC
Piscataway, NJ 08854

Cover design by Debbie O'Byrne at https://JetLaunch.net

Visit the author's website at www.ColleenGeorges.com

All rights reserved. No part of this publication may be reproduced, stored in a retrieval system, or transmitted in any form or by any means—for example, electronic, photocopy, recording—without the prior written permission of the publisher. The only exception is brief quotations in printed reviews.

Paperback ISBN-13: 978-1-7375281-1-1

RESCRIPT

Daily Gratitude Journal

Dr. Colleen Georges

Using the RESCRIPT Daily Gratitude Journal

The *RESCRIPT Daily Gratitude Journal* is all about helping you think thankfully so you can create abundance and joy into your life. Throughout your day, take a mental note of the experiences, people, actions/accomplishments, and sources/resources you feel thankful for. Allow yourself to really savor your grateful feelings from the moment you rise until the moment you round off your day.

Each night before you go to sleep, use the *RESCRIPT Daily Gratitude Journal* to write down the experiences, people, actions/accomplishments, and sources/resources you are grateful for that day. The items can be relatively small in importance (e.g., "my co-worker made the coffee today") or relatively large (e.g., "I earned a big promotion"). The goal is to remember a good experience, person, achievement, or resource in your life—then enjoy the good emotions that come with remembering.

The journal includes **365+ days** for you to savor what you are grateful for. It can be used on its own or as a companion to my 2019 award-winning book, *RESCRIPT the Story You're Telling Yourself*, which includes an in-depth chapter on Thinking Thankfully. **Every week begins with motivational quotes from inspiring people and brief revelations from gratitude research studies.**

Why Gratitude?

Within the field of Positive Psychology, gratitude is known as the queen of all virtues—often considered the antidote to what ails us mentally, emotionally, and even physically. In the year 2000, when I was struggling with anxiety, low self-esteem, panic attacks, and chronic neck, back, jaw pain, and headaches, I began a bedtime gratitude practice that eradicated these ailments and transformed my life. I've continued this practice to present day and began doing my evening practice with my son since 2014 when he was just five years old. I've experienced gratitude's positive impact in my life, my son's, my clients', and my students' lives. As a result, I've become a big advocate for the practice of gratitude.

Beginning and maintaining a bedtime gratitude practice is something I assign my clients regularly and the positive impact is remarkable. I've also assigned gratitude exercises as a professor and conducted my own research on its impact.

I taught a Positive Psychology-based course that incorporated several Positive Psychology exercises that students were asked to use in their professional and personal lives. One of the exercises I asked them to complete was to keep a Gratitude Journal for four weeks. Before going to sleep each night, I asked my students to write down three things they were grateful for from their day and to reflect on the experience at the end of the four weeks.

In reflecting upon keeping a Gratitude Journal for one month, students shared some amazing experiences. Coming up with things to be grateful for was difficult initially, however with daily practice it became hard *not* to do. My students cited noticing a new ability to appreciate little things they'd never thought about before and finding themselves thinking of their blessings readily throughout their day.

Practicing gratitude helped my students transform their perceptions of what they had thought was a bad day into viewing it as a good day. They found themselves suddenly looking for good in all things, even in unfortunate events, and diminishing episodes of negative rumination. They noted positive changes in the way they handled life's challenges. Reviewing what they were grateful for at night made them feel accomplished, as well as optimistic and excited about the next day, instead of stressed. Those who had struggled to fall or stay asleep began sleeping more quickly and soundly.

Gratitude exercises had lasting positive impacts on my students' relationships. Appreciating the kindness of others made them want to do more kind things for others and tell people how much they appreciated them. Loved ones even noted positive changes in my students' attitudes and demeanors after implementing gratitude practices into their lives.

Most students noted the gratitude exercises to be the most positively impactful activities in the course, and several students have shared with me in the years since that they have continued to use gratitude practices in their personal and professional lives. Furthermore, students reported experiencing increases in their overall life satisfaction, self-forgiveness, hope, life meaning, and gratitude.

Gratitude practices amplify our ability to think thankfully on a consistent basis, which has numerous positive impacts on our mental, emotional, and physical health and well-being in the short- and long-term.

RESCRIPT Gratitude Practices

Thank Your Treasures & Triumphs

Each of us has experiences, people, external resources, & personal strengths that are treasures in our lives, as well as experiences of triumph through achievement. These are blessings to feel thankful for. Take time to consider the people in your life that you are grateful for—friends, family, neighbors, pastor, mail carrier, doctor, hair stylist, restaurant server, or even a stranger you talked with at the supermarket. These individuals contribute to bringing you joy & comfort. What people in your life, positive experiences, external resources, & personal strengths & achievements are you thankful for?

Thank Your Trials & Tribulations

Each of us experience trials & tribulations in our lives—traumatic or challenging life experiences or losses of important relationships. The challenging experiences we face often provide us with some of the greatest wisdom & transformation in our lives. What challenging life experiences are you thankful for & why? People that are no longer in our lives still helped us to learn & grow in some way. We can decide to keep the good from them & let go of hurt & fear. What relationships that are no longer part of your life are you thankful for & why?

Celebrate Non-Catastrophes

This is an especially great gratitude practice for those who struggle with catastrophizing, because it takes care of enhancing two kinds of positive thinking at once! There are days when we feared a catastrophe or problem was going to happen, and then...it doesn't. This is a great thing to be thankful for—celebrate non-catastrophes! What catastrophes that never actually happened are you thankful for?

Recognize Others in Writing

In our lives there are often people we feel particularly thankful for. It could be someone who has had a positive impact in our lives like a family member, friend, mentor, colleague, or neighbor. We may feel thankful for those who provide a service to us in our daily lives, like a postal worker or doctor. How often do we give a proper thank you? A great way to express thanks is to recognize others in writing. You can write a comprehensive gratitude letter, a brief thank you email or text, a thank you card, or even post a post it note on the fridge for a family member or on a colleague's desk.

Kindle Kindness

Kindling Kindness in every area of our lives is a great way to say thank you to our higher power. When we show kindness to all living creatures and our planet, we express our gratitude to our higher power for everything that was created for us. Each day, make a practice of smiling at others, saying hello, & helping someone out in any way you can. Treat animals with love, care, & respect. Be good to the earth, keep it clean, pick up trash if you see it laying around, don't litter. These are just some small ways we can make a daily practice of thanking our higher power for everything that's been given to us.

Eradicate Envy

Social comparison is a soul killer. It's the breeder of envy. When we look around, we will always find someone who has something we don't have—a bigger house, fancier car, higher paying job, more close relationships. However, once we allow ourselves to look at all the blessings we do have & recognize that someone else's journey has its own unique treasures & tribulations, we can eradicate envy. When we eradicate envy, we free ourselves from its poison. We can celebrate others' treasures, while also having gratitude for our own gifts.

Compliments Instead of Complaints

When you find yourself desiring to complain or gossip about a person, do the opposite, the unthinkable—find a way to compliment the person instead! You can compliment the person directly by saying the compliment to them, or indirectly by saying it about them to someone else. This forces us to contemplate something good that we can appreciate in a person who doesn't generally illicit positive feelings within us. It's quite an effective strategy for growing gratitude and diminishing negative thoughts & feelings.

Talk Thankfully

To think thankfully, we must Talk Thankfully. If we spend a lot of time talking with others about the experiences, people, and things we perceive we are deprived of in our lives, we will think we are indeed deprived. We believe what we tell other people about our lives. However, if we focus on talking more about our blessings than our burdens, we begin to see our lives through a lens of abundance. Speak less of your deprivations & more of the good things in your life in your conversations with others. Then, watch the abundance you see in your life grow!

Acquire More Adventures Than Assets

When we focus more energy on acquiring adventures/experiences than on assets, we increase our joy & gratitude. This is because experiences have a longer lasting impact than things. We can recall the places, people, thrill, achievement, knowledge, skills, or other positive aspects & feelings associated with the experience long after it's over. Whereas the novelty & excitement of material things tends to wear off more quickly, leaving us seeking a new thing to make us feel fulfilled again. You don't have to banish buying things altogether. Just focus resources & energy on acquiring experiences—this will lead to a feeling of greater abundance!

Savor Each Second

We must train ourselves to savor each second. To engross ourselves in deep conversations. To listen more & talk less. To passionately embrace & feel the warmth of those we love. To profoundly see the radiant colors of the sky, grass, & trees. To intensely smell the fragrance of the flowers. To keenly taste the flavor of each bite of a meal. To acutely listen to the melody of the music & the meaning in the lyrics. We don't savor nearly enough. Instead, we multitask, we technologize, we stress & the now drifts right by. Let's make a practice of being present to savor each second, truly experience life & grow our awareness of all we have to be grateful for.

All-Around Life Appreciation Appraisal

Conduct a comprehensive appraisal of all you appreciate in your life to date. *In each area of your life, what experiences, people, achievements, and resources are you grateful for? What brings you happiness? Take a moment to truly savor these blessings and keep nurturing them!*

Relationships	
Career	
Financial	
Living Environment	
Community Engagement	
Physical Health	
Mental & Emotional Health	
Intellectual Growth	
Recreation & Relaxation	
Spirituality	

Think Thankfully!
Week #1

"Be thankful for what you have; you'll end up having more. If you concentrate on what you don't have, you will never, ever have enough."
~ Oprah Winfrey

Highlights From The Research:

Robert Emmons, the world's leading gratitude researcher, has found that those who engage in gratitude experience greater happiness, optimism, and alertness, and tend to be more forgiving, generous, and compassionate. Perhaps most intriguing, practicing gratitude is correlated with having a stronger immune system, lower blood pressure, and better sleep.[1]

Who Will You Express Your Gratitude To This Week?

_____
_____

Sunday _____
                        Date

Experiences I'm Grateful For Today (Events, Opportunities, Moments, & Sensations):
_____
_____
_____
_____

People I'm Grateful For Today (Interactions, Conversations, Kindnesses Given or Received):
_____
_____
_____
_____

Actions & Accomplishments I'm Grateful For Today (Big & Small):
_____
_____
_____
_____

Sources & Resources I'm Grateful For Today (Higher Power, Pets, Places, Things):
_____
_____
_____
_____

Monday _____
_{Date}

Experiences I'm Grateful For Today (Events, Opportunities, Moments, & Sensations):
_____
_____
_____

People I'm Grateful For Today (Interactions, Conversations, Kindnesses Given or Received):
_____
_____
_____

Actions & Accomplishments I'm Grateful For Today (Big & Small):
_____
_____
_____

Sources & Resources I'm Grateful For Today (Higher Power, Pets, Places, Things):
_____
_____
_____

Tuesday _____
Date

Experiences I'm Grateful For Today (Events, Opportunities, Moments, & Sensations):
_____
_____
_____

People I'm Grateful For Today (Interactions, Conversations, Kindnesses Given or Received):
_____
_____
_____

Actions & Accomplishments I'm Grateful For Today (Big & Small):
_____
_____
_____

Sources & Resources I'm Grateful For Today (Higher Power, Pets, Places, Things):
_____
_____
_____

Wednesday _____
_{Date}

Experiences I'm Grateful For Today (Events, Opportunities, Moments, & Sensations):
_____
_____
_____

People I'm Grateful For Today (Interactions, Conversations, Kindnesses Given or Received):
_____
_____
_____

Actions & Accomplishments I'm Grateful For Today (Big & Small):
_____
_____
_____

Sources & Resources I'm Grateful For Today (Higher Power, Pets, Places, Things):
_____
_____
_____

Thursday _____
_{Date}

Experiences I'm Grateful For Today (Events, Opportunities, Moments, & Sensations):
_____
_____
_____

People I'm Grateful For Today (Interactions, Conversations, Kindnesses Given or Received):
_____
_____
_____

Actions & Accomplishments I'm Grateful For Today (Big & Small):
_____
_____
_____

Sources & Resources I'm Grateful For Today (Higher Power, Pets, Places, Things):
_____
_____
_____

Friday _____
Date

Experiences I'm Grateful For Today (Events, Opportunities, Moments, & Sensations):
_____
_____
_____

People I'm Grateful For Today (Interactions, Conversations, Kindnesses Given or Received):
_____
_____
_____

Actions & Accomplishments I'm Grateful For Today (Big & Small):
_____
_____
_____

Sources & Resources I'm Grateful For Today (Higher Power, Pets, Places, Things):
_____
_____
_____

Saturday _____
Date

Experiences I'm Grateful For Today (Events, Opportunities, Moments, & Sensations):
_____
_____
_____

People I'm Grateful For Today (Interactions, Conversations, Kindnesses Given or Received):
_____
_____
_____

Actions & Accomplishments I'm Grateful For Today (Big & Small):
_____
_____
_____

Sources & Resources I'm Grateful For Today (Higher Power, Pets, Places, Things):
_____
_____
_____

Think Thankfully!
Week #2

"Gratitude unlocks the fullness of life. It turns what we have into enough, and more. It turns denial into acceptance, chaos to order, confusion to clarity. It can turn a meal into a feast, a house into a home, a stranger into a friend."
~ Melody Beattie

Highlights From The Research:

Seligman, Steen, Park, & Peterson found that those who wrote and delivered a letter of gratitude or kept a gratitude journal experienced both immediate and longer term increases in happiness and decreases in depression.[2]

Who Will You Express Your Gratitude To This Week?

_____
_____

Sunday _____
Date

Experiences I'm Grateful For Today (Events, Opportunities, Moments, & Sensations):
_____
_____
_____
_____

People I'm Grateful For Today (Interactions, Conversations, Kindnesses Given or Received):
_____
_____
_____
_____

Actions & Accomplishments I'm Grateful For Today (Big & Small):
_____
_____
_____
_____

Sources & Resources I'm Grateful For Today (Higher Power, Pets, Places, Things):
_____
_____
_____
_____

Monday _____
_____Date_____

Experiences I'm Grateful For Today (Events, Opportunities, Moments, & Sensations):
_____
_____
_____
_____

People I'm Grateful For Today (Interactions, Conversations, Kindnesses Given or Received):
_____
_____
_____
_____

Actions & Accomplishments I'm Grateful For Today (Big & Small):
_____
_____
_____
_____

Sources & Resources I'm Grateful For Today (Higher Power, Pets, Places, Things):
_____
_____
_____
_____

Tuesday _____
_____Date_____

Experiences I'm Grateful For Today (Events, Opportunities, Moments, & Sensations):
_____
_____
_____
_____

People I'm Grateful For Today (Interactions, Conversations, Kindnesses Given or Received):
_____
_____
_____
_____

Actions & Accomplishments I'm Grateful For Today (Big & Small):
_____
_____
_____
_____

Sources & Resources I'm Grateful For Today (Higher Power, Pets, Places, Things):
_____
_____
_____
_____

Wednesday _____
Date

Experiences I'm Grateful For Today (Events, Opportunities, Moments, & Sensations):
_____
_____
_____
_____

People I'm Grateful For Today (Interactions, Conversations, Kindnesses Given or Received):
_____
_____
_____
_____

Actions & Accomplishments I'm Grateful For Today (Big & Small):
_____
_____
_____
_____

Sources & Resources I'm Grateful For Today (Higher Power, Pets, Places, Things):
_____
_____
_____
_____

Thursday _____
Date

Experiences I'm Grateful For Today (Events, Opportunities, Moments, & Sensations):
_____
_____
_____
_____

People I'm Grateful For Today (Interactions, Conversations, Kindnesses Given or Received):
_____
_____
_____
_____

Actions & Accomplishments I'm Grateful For Today (Big & Small):
_____
_____
_____
_____

Sources & Resources I'm Grateful For Today (Higher Power, Pets, Places, Things):
_____
_____
_____
_____

Friday _____
_{Date}

Experiences I'm Grateful For Today (Events, Opportunities, Moments, & Sensations):
_____
_____
_____

People I'm Grateful For Today (Interactions, Conversations, Kindnesses Given or Received):
_____
_____
_____

Actions & Accomplishments I'm Grateful For Today (Big & Small):
_____
_____
_____

Sources & Resources I'm Grateful For Today (Higher Power, Pets, Places, Things):
_____
_____
_____

Saturday _____
_{Date}

Experiences I'm Grateful For Today (Events, Opportunities, Moments, & Sensations):
_____
_____
_____

People I'm Grateful For Today (Interactions, Conversations, Kindnesses Given or Received):
_____
_____
_____

Actions & Accomplishments I'm Grateful For Today (Big & Small):
_____
_____
_____

Sources & Resources I'm Grateful For Today (Higher Power, Pets, Places, Things):
_____
_____
_____

Think Thankfully!
Week #3

"It is impossible to feel grateful and depressed in the same moment."
~ Naomi Williams

Highlights From The Research:

Gordon, Arnette, & Smith conducted a study of couples and discovered that feeling and expressing gratitude is correlated with higher levels of marital satisfaction and happiness.[3]

Who Will You Express Your Gratitude To This Week?

_____
_____

Sunday _____
_____ Date

Experiences I'm Grateful For Today (Events, Opportunities, Moments, & Sensations):
_____
_____
_____
_____

People I'm Grateful For Today (Interactions, Conversations, Kindnesses Given or Received):
_____
_____
_____
_____

Actions & Accomplishments I'm Grateful For Today (Big & Small):
_____
_____
_____
_____

Sources & Resources I'm Grateful For Today (Higher Power, Pets, Places, Things):
_____
_____
_____
_____

Monday _____
_{Date}

Experiences I'm Grateful For Today (Events, Opportunities, Moments, & Sensations):
_____
_____
_____
_____

People I'm Grateful For Today (Interactions, Conversations, Kindnesses Given or Received):
_____
_____
_____
_____

Actions & Accomplishments I'm Grateful For Today (Big & Small):
_____
_____
_____
_____

Sources & Resources I'm Grateful For Today (Higher Power, Pets, Places, Things):
_____
_____
_____
_____

Tuesday _____
_{Date}

Experiences I'm Grateful For Today (Events, Opportunities, Moments, & Sensations):
_____
_____
_____
_____

People I'm Grateful For Today (Interactions, Conversations, Kindnesses Given or Received):
_____
_____
_____
_____

Actions & Accomplishments I'm Grateful For Today (Big & Small):
_____
_____
_____
_____

Sources & Resources I'm Grateful For Today (Higher Power, Pets, Places, Things):
_____
_____
_____
_____

Wednesday _____
Date

Experiences I'm Grateful For Today (Events, Opportunities, Moments, & Sensations):
_____
_____
_____

People I'm Grateful For Today (Interactions, Conversations, Kindnesses Given or Received):
_____
_____
_____
_____

Actions & Accomplishments I'm Grateful For Today (Big & Small):
_____
_____
_____
_____

Sources & Resources I'm Grateful For Today (Higher Power, Pets, Places, Things):
_____
_____
_____
_____

Thursday _____
Date

Experiences I'm Grateful For Today (Events, Opportunities, Moments, & Sensations):
_____
_____
_____

People I'm Grateful For Today (Interactions, Conversations, Kindnesses Given or Received):
_____
_____
_____
_____

Actions & Accomplishments I'm Grateful For Today (Big & Small):
_____
_____
_____
_____

Sources & Resources I'm Grateful For Today (Higher Power, Pets, Places, Things):
_____
_____
_____
_____

Friday _____
Date

Experiences I'm Grateful For Today (Events, Opportunities, Moments, & Sensations):
_____
_____
_____

People I'm Grateful For Today (Interactions, Conversations, Kindnesses Given or Received):
_____
_____
_____

Actions & Accomplishments I'm Grateful For Today (Big & Small):
_____
_____
_____

Sources & Resources I'm Grateful For Today (Higher Power, Pets, Places, Things):
_____
_____
_____

Saturday _____
Date

Experiences I'm Grateful For Today (Events, Opportunities, Moments, & Sensations):
_____
_____
_____

People I'm Grateful For Today (Interactions, Conversations, Kindnesses Given or Received):
_____
_____
_____

Actions & Accomplishments I'm Grateful For Today (Big & Small):
_____
_____
_____

Sources & Resources I'm Grateful For Today (Higher Power, Pets, Places, Things):
_____
_____
_____

Think Thankfully!
Week #4

"Gratitude is an antidote to negative emotions, a neutralizer of envy, hostility, worry, and irritation. It is savoring; it is not taking things for granted; it is present-oriented."
~ Sonja Lyubomirsky

Highlights From The Research:

Froh, Bono, Fan, Emmons, Henderson, and colleagues found that children who engaged in classroom-based gratitude activities, including keeping a gratitude journal, became more aware of how their thoughts impact their choices in social interactions, began to express gratitude more frequently, and were perceived by teachers to be happier.[4]

Who Will You Express Your Gratitude To This Week?

_____
_____

Sunday _____
Date

Experiences I'm Grateful For Today (Events, Opportunities, Moments, & Sensations):
_____
_____
_____
_____

People I'm Grateful For Today (Interactions, Conversations, Kindnesses Given or Received):
_____
_____
_____
_____

Actions & Accomplishments I'm Grateful For Today (Big & Small):
_____
_____
_____
_____

Sources & Resources I'm Grateful For Today (Higher Power, Pets, Places, Things):
_____
_____
_____
_____

Monday _____
Date

Experiences I'm Grateful For Today (Events, Opportunities, Moments, & Sensations):
_____
_____
_____
_____

People I'm Grateful For Today (Interactions, Conversations, Kindnesses Given or Received):
_____
_____
_____
_____

Actions & Accomplishments I'm Grateful For Today (Big & Small):
_____
_____
_____
_____

Sources & Resources I'm Grateful For Today (Higher Power, Pets, Places, Things):
_____
_____
_____
_____

Tuesday _____
Date

Experiences I'm Grateful For Today (Events, Opportunities, Moments, & Sensations):
_____
_____
_____
_____

People I'm Grateful For Today (Interactions, Conversations, Kindnesses Given or Received):
_____
_____
_____
_____

Actions & Accomplishments I'm Grateful For Today (Big & Small):
_____
_____
_____
_____

Sources & Resources I'm Grateful For Today (Higher Power, Pets, Places, Things):
_____
_____
_____
_____

Wednesday _____
Date

Experiences I'm Grateful For Today (Events, Opportunities, Moments, & Sensations):
_____
_____
_____

People I'm Grateful For Today (Interactions, Conversations, Kindnesses Given or Received):
_____
_____
_____
_____

Actions & Accomplishments I'm Grateful For Today (Big & Small):
_____
_____
_____
_____

Sources & Resources I'm Grateful For Today (Higher Power, Pets, Places, Things):
_____
_____
_____
_____

Thursday _____
Date

Experiences I'm Grateful For Today (Events, Opportunities, Moments, & Sensations):
_____
_____
_____

People I'm Grateful For Today (Interactions, Conversations, Kindnesses Given or Received):
_____
_____
_____
_____

Actions & Accomplishments I'm Grateful For Today (Big & Small):
_____
_____
_____
_____

Sources & Resources I'm Grateful For Today (Higher Power, Pets, Places, Things):
_____
_____
_____
_____

Friday _____
_{Date}

Experiences I'm Grateful For Today (Events, Opportunities, Moments, & Sensations):
_____
_____
_____

People I'm Grateful For Today (Interactions, Conversations, Kindnesses Given or Received):
_____
_____
_____

Actions & Accomplishments I'm Grateful For Today (Big & Small):
_____
_____
_____

Sources & Resources I'm Grateful For Today (Higher Power, Pets, Places, Things):
_____
_____
_____

Saturday _____
_{Date}

Experiences I'm Grateful For Today (Events, Opportunities, Moments, & Sensations):
_____
_____
_____

People I'm Grateful For Today (Interactions, Conversations, Kindnesses Given or Received):
_____
_____
_____

Actions & Accomplishments I'm Grateful For Today (Big & Small):
_____
_____
_____

Sources & Resources I'm Grateful For Today (Higher Power, Pets, Places, Things):
_____
_____
_____

Think Thankfully!
Week #5

"Gratitude is an art of painting an adversity into a lovely picture."
~ Kak Sri

Highlights From The Research:

Bartlett & Arpin conducted a study of older adults who completed a three-week gratitude intervention, listing three good things that happened that day before bedtime, and found that practicing gratitude decreased feelings of loneliness and boosted self-reported health and well-being.[5]

Who Will You Express Your Gratitude To This Week?
_____
_____

Sunday _____
                                    Date

Experiences I'm Grateful For Today (Events, Opportunities, Moments, & Sensations):
_____
_____
_____
_____

People I'm Grateful For Today (Interactions, Conversations, Kindnesses Given or Received):
_____
_____
_____
_____

Actions & Accomplishments I'm Grateful For Today (Big & Small):
_____
_____
_____
_____

Sources & Resources I'm Grateful For Today (Higher Power, Pets, Places, Things):
_____
_____
_____
_____

Monday _____
Date

Experiences I'm Grateful For Today (Events, Opportunities, Moments, & Sensations):
_____
_____
_____

People I'm Grateful For Today (Interactions, Conversations, Kindnesses Given or Received):
_____
_____
_____
_____

Actions & Accomplishments I'm Grateful For Today (Big & Small):
_____
_____
_____
_____

Sources & Resources I'm Grateful For Today (Higher Power, Pets, Places, Things):
_____
_____
_____
_____

Tuesday _____
Date

Experiences I'm Grateful For Today (Events, Opportunities, Moments, & Sensations):
_____
_____
_____

People I'm Grateful For Today (Interactions, Conversations, Kindnesses Given or Received):
_____
_____
_____
_____

Actions & Accomplishments I'm Grateful For Today (Big & Small):
_____
_____
_____
_____

Sources & Resources I'm Grateful For Today (Higher Power, Pets, Places, Things):
_____
_____
_____
_____

Wednesday _____
Date

Experiences I'm Grateful For Today (Events, Opportunities, Moments, & Sensations):
_____
_____
_____

People I'm Grateful For Today (Interactions, Conversations, Kindnesses Given or Received):
_____
_____
_____
_____

Actions & Accomplishments I'm Grateful For Today (Big & Small):
_____
_____
_____
_____

Sources & Resources I'm Grateful For Today (Higher Power, Pets, Places, Things):
_____
_____
_____
_____

Thursday _____
Date

Experiences I'm Grateful For Today (Events, Opportunities, Moments, & Sensations):
_____
_____
_____

People I'm Grateful For Today (Interactions, Conversations, Kindnesses Given or Received):
_____
_____
_____
_____

Actions & Accomplishments I'm Grateful For Today (Big & Small):
_____
_____
_____
_____

Sources & Resources I'm Grateful For Today (Higher Power, Pets, Places, Things):
_____
_____
_____
_____

Friday _____
_{Date}

Experiences I'm Grateful For Today (Events, Opportunities, Moments, & Sensations):
_____
_____
_____

People I'm Grateful For Today (Interactions, Conversations, Kindnesses Given or Received):
_____
_____
_____

Actions & Accomplishments I'm Grateful For Today (Big & Small):
_____
_____
_____

Sources & Resources I'm Grateful For Today (Higher Power, Pets, Places, Things):
_____
_____
_____

Saturday _____
_{Date}

Experiences I'm Grateful For Today (Events, Opportunities, Moments, & Sensations):
_____
_____
_____

People I'm Grateful For Today (Interactions, Conversations, Kindnesses Given or Received):
_____
_____
_____

Actions & Accomplishments I'm Grateful For Today (Big & Small):
_____
_____
_____

Sources & Resources I'm Grateful For Today (Higher Power, Pets, Places, Things):
_____
_____
_____

Think Thankfully!
Week #6

"What separates privilege from entitlement is gratitude."
~ Brené Brown

Highlights From The Research:

Krejtz, Nezlek, Michnicka, Holas, & Rusanowska performed a study of adults who journaled up to six things they were grateful for daily for two weeks and discovered that counting one's blessing can reduce the negative impact of daily stressors.[6]

Who Will You Express Your Gratitude To This Week?

_____
_____

Sunday _____
                              Date

Experiences I'm Grateful For Today (Events, Opportunities, Moments, & Sensations):
_____
_____
_____
_____

People I'm Grateful For Today (Interactions, Conversations, Kindnesses Given or Received):
_____
_____
_____
_____

Actions & Accomplishments I'm Grateful For Today (Big & Small):
_____
_____
_____
_____

Sources & Resources I'm Grateful For Today (Higher Power, Pets, Places, Things):
_____
_____
_____
_____

Monday _____
Date

Experiences I'm Grateful For Today (Events, Opportunities, Moments, & Sensations):
_____
_____
_____

People I'm Grateful For Today (Interactions, Conversations, Kindnesses Given or Received):
_____
_____
_____

Actions & Accomplishments I'm Grateful For Today (Big & Small):
_____
_____
_____

Sources & Resources I'm Grateful For Today (Higher Power, Pets, Places, Things):
_____
_____
_____

Tuesday _____
Date

Experiences I'm Grateful For Today (Events, Opportunities, Moments, & Sensations):
_____
_____
_____

People I'm Grateful For Today (Interactions, Conversations, Kindnesses Given or Received):
_____
_____
_____

Actions & Accomplishments I'm Grateful For Today (Big & Small):
_____
_____
_____

Sources & Resources I'm Grateful For Today (Higher Power, Pets, Places, Things):
_____
_____
_____

Wednesday _____
_{Date}

Experiences I'm Grateful For Today (Events, Opportunities, Moments, & Sensations):
_____
_____
_____

People I'm Grateful For Today (Interactions, Conversations, Kindnesses Given or Received):
_____
_____
_____
_____

Actions & Accomplishments I'm Grateful For Today (Big & Small):
_____
_____
_____
_____

Sources & Resources I'm Grateful For Today (Higher Power, Pets, Places, Things):
_____
_____
_____

Thursday _____
_{Date}

Experiences I'm Grateful For Today (Events, Opportunities, Moments, & Sensations):
_____
_____
_____

People I'm Grateful For Today (Interactions, Conversations, Kindnesses Given or Received):
_____
_____
_____
_____

Actions & Accomplishments I'm Grateful For Today (Big & Small):
_____
_____
_____
_____

Sources & Resources I'm Grateful For Today (Higher Power, Pets, Places, Things):
_____
_____
_____

Friday _____
_{Date}

Experiences I'm Grateful For Today (Events, Opportunities, Moments, & Sensations):
_____
_____
_____

People I'm Grateful For Today (Interactions, Conversations, Kindnesses Given or Received):
_____
_____
_____

Actions & Accomplishments I'm Grateful For Today (Big & Small):
_____
_____
_____

Sources & Resources I'm Grateful For Today (Higher Power, Pets, Places, Things):
_____
_____
_____

Saturday _____
_{Date}

Experiences I'm Grateful For Today (Events, Opportunities, Moments, & Sensations):
_____
_____
_____

People I'm Grateful For Today (Interactions, Conversations, Kindnesses Given or Received):
_____
_____
_____

Actions & Accomplishments I'm Grateful For Today (Big & Small):
_____
_____
_____

Sources & Resources I'm Grateful For Today (Higher Power, Pets, Places, Things):
_____
_____
_____

Think Thankfully!
Week #7

"When we focus on our gratitude, the tide of disappointment goes out and the tide of love rushes in."
~ Kristin Armstrong

Highlights From The Research:

Digdon & Koble conducted a study of college students who participated in a one-week gratitude practice, journaling about a recent or anticipated positive event daily, and uncovered that practicing gratitude reduces worry and pre-sleep stimulation and improves sleep.[7]

Who Will You Express Your Gratitude To This Week?

_____
_____

Sunday _____
                                        Date

Experiences I'm Grateful For Today (Events, Opportunities, Moments, & Sensations):
_____
_____
_____
_____

People I'm Grateful For Today (Interactions, Conversations, Kindnesses Given or Received):
_____
_____
_____
_____

Actions & Accomplishments I'm Grateful For Today (Big & Small):
_____
_____
_____
_____

Sources & Resources I'm Grateful For Today (Higher Power, Pets, Places, Things):
_____
_____
_____
_____

Monday _____
<small>Date</small>

Experiences I'm Grateful For Today (Events, Opportunities, Moments, & Sensations):
_____
_____
_____
_____

People I'm Grateful For Today (Interactions, Conversations, Kindnesses Given or Received):
_____
_____
_____
_____

Actions & Accomplishments I'm Grateful For Today (Big & Small):
_____
_____
_____
_____

Sources & Resources I'm Grateful For Today (Higher Power, Pets, Places, Things):
_____
_____
_____
_____

Tuesday _____
<small>Date</small>

Experiences I'm Grateful For Today (Events, Opportunities, Moments, & Sensations):
_____
_____
_____
_____

People I'm Grateful For Today (Interactions, Conversations, Kindnesses Given or Received):
_____
_____
_____
_____

Actions & Accomplishments I'm Grateful For Today (Big & Small):
_____
_____
_____
_____

Sources & Resources I'm Grateful For Today (Higher Power, Pets, Places, Things):
_____
_____
_____
_____

Wednesday _____
Date

Experiences I'm Grateful For Today (Events, Opportunities, Moments, & Sensations):
_____
_____
_____

People I'm Grateful For Today (Interactions, Conversations, Kindnesses Given or Received):
_____
_____
_____

Actions & Accomplishments I'm Grateful For Today (Big & Small):
_____
_____
_____

Sources & Resources I'm Grateful For Today (Higher Power, Pets, Places, Things):
_____
_____
_____

Thursday _____
Date

Experiences I'm Grateful For Today (Events, Opportunities, Moments, & Sensations):
_____
_____
_____

People I'm Grateful For Today (Interactions, Conversations, Kindnesses Given or Received):
_____
_____
_____

Actions & Accomplishments I'm Grateful For Today (Big & Small):
_____
_____
_____

Sources & Resources I'm Grateful For Today (Higher Power, Pets, Places, Things):
_____
_____
_____

Friday _____
Date

Experiences I'm Grateful For Today (Events, Opportunities, Moments, & Sensations):
_____
_____
_____

People I'm Grateful For Today (Interactions, Conversations, Kindnesses Given or Received):
_____
_____
_____

Actions & Accomplishments I'm Grateful For Today (Big & Small):
_____
_____
_____

Sources & Resources I'm Grateful For Today (Higher Power, Pets, Places, Things):
_____
_____
_____

Saturday _____
Date

Experiences I'm Grateful For Today (Events, Opportunities, Moments, & Sensations):
_____
_____
_____

People I'm Grateful For Today (Interactions, Conversations, Kindnesses Given or Received):
_____
_____
_____

Actions & Accomplishments I'm Grateful For Today (Big & Small):
_____
_____
_____

Sources & Resources I'm Grateful For Today (Higher Power, Pets, Places, Things):
_____
_____
_____

Think Thankfully!
Week #8

"Gratitude is an opener of locked-up blessings."
~ Marianne Williamson

Highlights From The Research:

Kashdan, Uswatte, & Julian examined the relationship between gratitude and well-being in combat veterans with and without PTSD. The study found that dispositional gratitude was correlated with greater daily positive emotions, a higher percentage of reported pleasant days, more daily intrinsically motivating activity, and higher daily self-esteem.[8]

Who Will You Express Your Gratitude To This Week?
_____
_____

Sunday _____
                           Date

Experiences I'm Grateful For Today (Events, Opportunities, Moments, & Sensations):
_____
_____
_____
_____

People I'm Grateful For Today (Interactions, Conversations, Kindnesses Given or Received):
_____
_____
_____
_____

Actions & Accomplishments I'm Grateful For Today (Big & Small):
_____
_____
_____
_____

Sources & Resources I'm Grateful For Today (Higher Power, Pets, Places, Things):
_____
_____
_____
_____

Monday _____
_{Date}

Experiences I'm Grateful For Today (Events, Opportunities, Moments, & Sensations):
_____
_____
_____

People I'm Grateful For Today (Interactions, Conversations, Kindnesses Given or Received):
_____
_____
_____

Actions & Accomplishments I'm Grateful For Today (Big & Small):
_____
_____
_____

Sources & Resources I'm Grateful For Today (Higher Power, Pets, Places, Things):
_____
_____
_____

Tuesday _____
_{Date}

Experiences I'm Grateful For Today (Events, Opportunities, Moments, & Sensations):
_____
_____
_____

People I'm Grateful For Today (Interactions, Conversations, Kindnesses Given or Received):
_____
_____
_____

Actions & Accomplishments I'm Grateful For Today (Big & Small):
_____
_____
_____

Sources & Resources I'm Grateful For Today (Higher Power, Pets, Places, Things):
_____
_____
_____

Wednesday _____
_{Date}

Experiences I'm Grateful For Today (Events, Opportunities, Moments, & Sensations):
_____
_____
_____
_____

People I'm Grateful For Today (Interactions, Conversations, Kindnesses Given or Received):
_____
_____
_____
_____

Actions & Accomplishments I'm Grateful For Today (Big & Small):
_____
_____
_____
_____

Sources & Resources I'm Grateful For Today (Higher Power, Pets, Places, Things):
_____
_____
_____
_____

Thursday _____
_{Date}

Experiences I'm Grateful For Today (Events, Opportunities, Moments, & Sensations):
_____
_____
_____
_____

People I'm Grateful For Today (Interactions, Conversations, Kindnesses Given or Received):
_____
_____
_____
_____

Actions & Accomplishments I'm Grateful For Today (Big & Small):
_____
_____
_____
_____

Sources & Resources I'm Grateful For Today (Higher Power, Pets, Places, Things):
_____
_____
_____
_____

Friday _____
_{Date}

Experiences I'm Grateful For Today (Events, Opportunities, Moments, & Sensations):
_____
_____
_____

People I'm Grateful For Today (Interactions, Conversations, Kindnesses Given or Received):
_____
_____
_____

Actions & Accomplishments I'm Grateful For Today (Big & Small):
_____
_____
_____

Sources & Resources I'm Grateful For Today (Higher Power, Pets, Places, Things):
_____
_____
_____

Saturday _____
_{Date}

Experiences I'm Grateful For Today (Events, Opportunities, Moments, & Sensations):
_____
_____
_____

People I'm Grateful For Today (Interactions, Conversations, Kindnesses Given or Received):
_____
_____
_____

Actions & Accomplishments I'm Grateful For Today (Big & Small):
_____
_____
_____

Sources & Resources I'm Grateful For Today (Higher Power, Pets, Places, Things):
_____
_____
_____

Think Thankfully!
Week #9

"Let gratitude be the pillow upon which you kneel to say your nightly prayer."
~ Maya Angelou

Highlights From The Research:

Heckendorf, Lehr, Ebert, & Freund performed a study of adults who participated in a five-week gratitude intervention involving weekly online gratitude training sessions and daily use of a mobile gratitude app that involved taking pictures or notes of positive moments during the day and recalling positive moments and their sources in the evening. They found that practicing gratitude reduces repetitive negative thinking, anxiety, depression, and insomnia.[9]

Who Will You Express Your Gratitude To This Week?

_____
_____

Sunday _____
                            Date

Experiences I'm Grateful For Today (Events, Opportunities, Moments, & Sensations):
_____
_____
_____
_____

People I'm Grateful For Today (Interactions, Conversations, Kindnesses Given or Received):
_____
_____
_____
_____

Actions & Accomplishments I'm Grateful For Today (Big & Small):
_____
_____
_____
_____

Sources & Resources I'm Grateful For Today (Higher Power, Pets, Places, Things):
_____
_____
_____
_____

Monday _____
Date

Experiences I'm Grateful For Today (Events, Opportunities, Moments, & Sensations):
_____
_____
_____

People I'm Grateful For Today (Interactions, Conversations, Kindnesses Given or Received):
_____
_____
_____
_____

Actions & Accomplishments I'm Grateful For Today (Big & Small):
_____
_____
_____
_____

Sources & Resources I'm Grateful For Today (Higher Power, Pets, Places, Things):
_____
_____
_____
_____

Tuesday _____
Date

Experiences I'm Grateful For Today (Events, Opportunities, Moments, & Sensations):
_____
_____
_____

People I'm Grateful For Today (Interactions, Conversations, Kindnesses Given or Received):
_____
_____
_____
_____

Actions & Accomplishments I'm Grateful For Today (Big & Small):
_____
_____
_____
_____

Sources & Resources I'm Grateful For Today (Higher Power, Pets, Places, Things):
_____
_____
_____
_____

Wednesday _____
Date

Experiences I'm Grateful For Today (Events, Opportunities, Moments, & Sensations):
_____
_____
_____

People I'm Grateful For Today (Interactions, Conversations, Kindnesses Given or Received):
_____
_____
_____

Actions & Accomplishments I'm Grateful For Today (Big & Small):
_____
_____
_____

Sources & Resources I'm Grateful For Today (Higher Power, Pets, Places, Things):
_____
_____
_____

Thursday _____
Date

Experiences I'm Grateful For Today (Events, Opportunities, Moments, & Sensations):
_____
_____
_____

People I'm Grateful For Today (Interactions, Conversations, Kindnesses Given or Received):
_____
_____
_____

Actions & Accomplishments I'm Grateful For Today (Big & Small):
_____
_____
_____

Sources & Resources I'm Grateful For Today (Higher Power, Pets, Places, Things):
_____
_____
_____

Friday _____
_{Date}

Experiences I'm Grateful For Today (Events, Opportunities, Moments, & Sensations):
_____
_____
_____
_____

People I'm Grateful For Today (Interactions, Conversations, Kindnesses Given or Received):
_____
_____
_____
_____

Actions & Accomplishments I'm Grateful For Today (Big & Small):
_____
_____
_____
_____

Sources & Resources I'm Grateful For Today (Higher Power, Pets, Places, Things):
_____
_____
_____
_____

Saturday _____
_{Date}

Experiences I'm Grateful For Today (Events, Opportunities, Moments, & Sensations):
_____
_____
_____
_____

People I'm Grateful For Today (Interactions, Conversations, Kindnesses Given or Received):
_____
_____
_____
_____

Actions & Accomplishments I'm Grateful For Today (Big & Small):
_____
_____
_____
_____

Sources & Resources I'm Grateful For Today (Higher Power, Pets, Places, Things):
_____
_____
_____
_____

Think Thankfully!
Week #10

"We must find time to stop and thank the people who make a difference in our lives."
~ John F. Kennedy

Highlights From The Research:

Kaplan, Bradley-Geist, Ahmad, Anderson, Hargrove, & Lindsey studied university employees who participated in a two-week gratitude intervention that involved listing things they were grateful for about their job at least three times a week. They found that gratitude led to increased intensity and frequency of positive emotions and a decrease in illness-related work absences.[10]

Who Will You Express Your Gratitude To This Week?
_____
_____

Sunday _____
_____Date

Experiences I'm Grateful For Today (Events, Opportunities, Moments, & Sensations):
_____
_____
_____
_____

People I'm Grateful For Today (Interactions, Conversations, Kindnesses Given or Received):
_____
_____
_____
_____

Actions & Accomplishments I'm Grateful For Today (Big & Small):
_____
_____
_____
_____

Sources & Resources I'm Grateful For Today (Higher Power, Pets, Places, Things):
_____
_____
_____
_____

Monday _____
Date

Experiences I'm Grateful For Today (Events, Opportunities, Moments, & Sensations):
_____
_____
_____

People I'm Grateful For Today (Interactions, Conversations, Kindnesses Given or Received):
_____
_____
_____
_____

Actions & Accomplishments I'm Grateful For Today (Big & Small):
_____
_____
_____
_____

Sources & Resources I'm Grateful For Today (Higher Power, Pets, Places, Things):
_____
_____
_____
_____

Tuesday _____
Date

Experiences I'm Grateful For Today (Events, Opportunities, Moments, & Sensations):
_____
_____
_____

People I'm Grateful For Today (Interactions, Conversations, Kindnesses Given or Received):
_____
_____
_____
_____

Actions & Accomplishments I'm Grateful For Today (Big & Small):
_____
_____
_____
_____

Sources & Resources I'm Grateful For Today (Higher Power, Pets, Places, Things):
_____
_____
_____
_____

Wednesday _____
Date

Experiences I'm Grateful For Today (Events, Opportunities, Moments, & Sensations):
_____
_____
_____

People I'm Grateful For Today (Interactions, Conversations, Kindnesses Given or Received):
_____
_____
_____

Actions & Accomplishments I'm Grateful For Today (Big & Small):
_____
_____
_____

Sources & Resources I'm Grateful For Today (Higher Power, Pets, Places, Things):
_____
_____
_____

Thursday _____
Date

Experiences I'm Grateful For Today (Events, Opportunities, Moments, & Sensations):
_____
_____
_____

People I'm Grateful For Today (Interactions, Conversations, Kindnesses Given or Received):
_____
_____
_____

Actions & Accomplishments I'm Grateful For Today (Big & Small):
_____
_____
_____

Sources & Resources I'm Grateful For Today (Higher Power, Pets, Places, Things):
_____
_____
_____

Friday _____
_{Date}

Experiences I'm Grateful For Today (Events, Opportunities, Moments, & Sensations):
_____
_____
_____

People I'm Grateful For Today (Interactions, Conversations, Kindnesses Given or Received):
_____
_____
_____

Actions & Accomplishments I'm Grateful For Today (Big & Small):
_____
_____
_____

Sources & Resources I'm Grateful For Today (Higher Power, Pets, Places, Things):
_____
_____
_____

Saturday _____
_{Date}

Experiences I'm Grateful For Today (Events, Opportunities, Moments, & Sensations):
_____
_____
_____

People I'm Grateful For Today (Interactions, Conversations, Kindnesses Given or Received):
_____
_____
_____

Actions & Accomplishments I'm Grateful For Today (Big & Small):
_____
_____
_____

Sources & Resources I'm Grateful For Today (Higher Power, Pets, Places, Things):
_____
_____
_____

Think Thankfully!
Week #11

"Take full account of what Excellencies you possess, and in gratitude remember how you would hanker after them, if you had them not."
~ Marcus Aurelius

Highlights From The Research:

Kyeong, Kim, Kim, Kim, & Kim studied adults who participated in a gratitude meditation and found that when participants mentally focused on things they were grateful for their heart rates lowered and calmed and communication between regions of the brain associated with increased anxiety relaxed, facilitating positive emotional regulation.[11]

Who Will You Express Your Gratitude To This Week?

_____
_____

Sunday _____
Date

Experiences I'm Grateful For Today (Events, Opportunities, Moments, & Sensations):
_____
_____
_____
_____

People I'm Grateful For Today (Interactions, Conversations, Kindnesses Given or Received):
_____
_____
_____
_____

Actions & Accomplishments I'm Grateful For Today (Big & Small):
_____
_____
_____
_____

Sources & Resources I'm Grateful For Today (Higher Power, Pets, Places, Things):
_____
_____
_____
_____

Monday _____
Date

Experiences I'm Grateful For Today (Events, Opportunities, Moments, & Sensations):
_____
_____
_____
_____

People I'm Grateful For Today (Interactions, Conversations, Kindnesses Given or Received):
_____
_____
_____
_____

Actions & Accomplishments I'm Grateful For Today (Big & Small):
_____
_____
_____
_____

Sources & Resources I'm Grateful For Today (Higher Power, Pets, Places, Things):
_____
_____
_____
_____

Tuesday _____
Date

Experiences I'm Grateful For Today (Events, Opportunities, Moments, & Sensations):
_____
_____
_____
_____

People I'm Grateful For Today (Interactions, Conversations, Kindnesses Given or Received):
_____
_____
_____
_____

Actions & Accomplishments I'm Grateful For Today (Big & Small):
_____
_____
_____
_____

Sources & Resources I'm Grateful For Today (Higher Power, Pets, Places, Things):
_____
_____
_____
_____

Wednesday _____
Date

Experiences I'm Grateful For Today (Events, Opportunities, Moments, & Sensations):
_____
_____
_____

People I'm Grateful For Today (Interactions, Conversations, Kindnesses Given or Received):
_____
_____
_____

Actions & Accomplishments I'm Grateful For Today (Big & Small):
_____
_____
_____

Sources & Resources I'm Grateful For Today (Higher Power, Pets, Places, Things):
_____
_____
_____

Thursday _____
Date

Experiences I'm Grateful For Today (Events, Opportunities, Moments, & Sensations):
_____
_____
_____

People I'm Grateful For Today (Interactions, Conversations, Kindnesses Given or Received):
_____
_____
_____

Actions & Accomplishments I'm Grateful For Today (Big & Small):
_____
_____
_____

Sources & Resources I'm Grateful For Today (Higher Power, Pets, Places, Things):
_____
_____
_____

Friday _____
Date

Experiences I'm Grateful For Today (Events, Opportunities, Moments, & Sensations):
_____
_____
_____

People I'm Grateful For Today (Interactions, Conversations, Kindnesses Given or Received):
_____
_____
_____

Actions & Accomplishments I'm Grateful For Today (Big & Small):
_____
_____
_____

Sources & Resources I'm Grateful For Today (Higher Power, Pets, Places, Things):
_____
_____
_____

Saturday _____
Date

Experiences I'm Grateful For Today (Events, Opportunities, Moments, & Sensations):
_____
_____
_____

People I'm Grateful For Today (Interactions, Conversations, Kindnesses Given or Received):
_____
_____
_____

Actions & Accomplishments I'm Grateful For Today (Big & Small):
_____
_____
_____

Sources & Resources I'm Grateful For Today (Higher Power, Pets, Places, Things):
_____
_____
_____

Think Thankfully!
Week #12

"Gratitude is the foundation of compassion."
~ Master Jun Hong Lu

Highlights From The Research:

DeWall, Lambert, Pond, Kashdan, & Fincham conducted a study of college students who wrote a letter about five things in their lives they were most grateful for and found that concentrating on gratitude facilitated reduced anger and aggression.[12]

Who Will You Express Your Gratitude To This Week?

_____
_____

Sunday _____
                    Date

Experiences I'm Grateful For Today (Events, Opportunities, Moments, & Sensations):
_____
_____
_____
_____

People I'm Grateful For Today (Interactions, Conversations, Kindnesses Given or Received):
_____
_____
_____
_____

Actions & Accomplishments I'm Grateful For Today (Big & Small):
_____
_____
_____
_____

Sources & Resources I'm Grateful For Today (Higher Power, Pets, Places, Things):
_____
_____
_____
_____

Monday _____
Date

Experiences I'm Grateful For Today (Events, Opportunities, Moments, & Sensations):
_____
_____
_____

People I'm Grateful For Today (Interactions, Conversations, Kindnesses Given or Received):
_____
_____
_____

Actions & Accomplishments I'm Grateful For Today (Big & Small):
_____
_____
_____

Sources & Resources I'm Grateful For Today (Higher Power, Pets, Places, Things):
_____
_____
_____

Tuesday _____
Date

Experiences I'm Grateful For Today (Events, Opportunities, Moments, & Sensations):
_____
_____
_____

People I'm Grateful For Today (Interactions, Conversations, Kindnesses Given or Received):
_____
_____
_____

Actions & Accomplishments I'm Grateful For Today (Big & Small):
_____
_____
_____

Sources & Resources I'm Grateful For Today (Higher Power, Pets, Places, Things):
_____
_____
_____

Wednesday _____
Date

Experiences I'm Grateful For Today (Events, Opportunities, Moments, & Sensations):
_____
_____
_____

People I'm Grateful For Today (Interactions, Conversations, Kindnesses Given or Received):
_____
_____
_____
_____

Actions & Accomplishments I'm Grateful For Today (Big & Small):
_____
_____
_____
_____

Sources & Resources I'm Grateful For Today (Higher Power, Pets, Places, Things):
_____
_____
_____
_____

Thursday _____
Date

Experiences I'm Grateful For Today (Events, Opportunities, Moments, & Sensations):
_____
_____
_____

People I'm Grateful For Today (Interactions, Conversations, Kindnesses Given or Received):
_____
_____
_____
_____

Actions & Accomplishments I'm Grateful For Today (Big & Small):
_____
_____
_____
_____

Sources & Resources I'm Grateful For Today (Higher Power, Pets, Places, Things):
_____
_____
_____
_____

Friday _____
_{Date}

Experiences I'm Grateful For Today (Events, Opportunities, Moments, & Sensations):
_____
_____
_____

People I'm Grateful For Today (Interactions, Conversations, Kindnesses Given or Received):
_____
_____
_____

Actions & Accomplishments I'm Grateful For Today (Big & Small):
_____
_____
_____

Sources & Resources I'm Grateful For Today (Higher Power, Pets, Places, Things):
_____
_____
_____

Saturday _____
_{Date}

Experiences I'm Grateful For Today (Events, Opportunities, Moments, & Sensations):
_____
_____
_____

People I'm Grateful For Today (Interactions, Conversations, Kindnesses Given or Received):
_____
_____
_____

Actions & Accomplishments I'm Grateful For Today (Big & Small):
_____
_____
_____

Sources & Resources I'm Grateful For Today (Higher Power, Pets, Places, Things):
_____
_____
_____

Think Thankfully!
Week #13

*"Appreciation can make a day - even change a life.
Your willingness to put it into words is all that is necessary."
~ Margaret Cousins*

Highlights From The Research:

Froh, Sefick, & Emmons studied early adolescents who listed five things they were grateful for five times a week for two weeks and found that counting blessings was correlated with increased optimism, life satisfaction, and decreased negative emotions.[13]

Who Will You Express Your Gratitude To This Week?

_____
_____

Sunday _____
                    Date

Experiences I'm Grateful For Today (Events, Opportunities, Moments, & Sensations):
_____
_____
_____
_____

People I'm Grateful For Today (Interactions, Conversations, Kindnesses Given or Received):
_____
_____
_____
_____

Actions & Accomplishments I'm Grateful For Today (Big & Small):
_____
_____
_____
_____

Sources & Resources I'm Grateful For Today (Higher Power, Pets, Places, Things):
_____
_____
_____
_____

Monday _____
Date

Experiences I'm Grateful For Today (Events, Opportunities, Moments, & Sensations):
_____
_____
_____
_____

People I'm Grateful For Today (Interactions, Conversations, Kindnesses Given or Received):
_____
_____
_____
_____

Actions & Accomplishments I'm Grateful For Today (Big & Small):
_____
_____
_____
_____

Sources & Resources I'm Grateful For Today (Higher Power, Pets, Places, Things):
_____
_____
_____
_____

Tuesday _____
Date

Experiences I'm Grateful For Today (Events, Opportunities, Moments, & Sensations):
_____
_____
_____
_____

People I'm Grateful For Today (Interactions, Conversations, Kindnesses Given or Received):
_____
_____
_____
_____

Actions & Accomplishments I'm Grateful For Today (Big & Small):
_____
_____
_____
_____

Sources & Resources I'm Grateful For Today (Higher Power, Pets, Places, Things):
_____
_____
_____
_____

Wednesday _____
Date

Experiences I'm Grateful For Today (Events, Opportunities, Moments, & Sensations):
_____
_____
_____

People I'm Grateful For Today (Interactions, Conversations, Kindnesses Given or Received):
_____
_____
_____

Actions & Accomplishments I'm Grateful For Today (Big & Small):
_____
_____
_____

Sources & Resources I'm Grateful For Today (Higher Power, Pets, Places, Things):
_____
_____
_____

Thursday _____
Date

Experiences I'm Grateful For Today (Events, Opportunities, Moments, & Sensations):
_____
_____
_____

People I'm Grateful For Today (Interactions, Conversations, Kindnesses Given or Received):
_____
_____
_____

Actions & Accomplishments I'm Grateful For Today (Big & Small):
_____
_____
_____

Sources & Resources I'm Grateful For Today (Higher Power, Pets, Places, Things):
_____
_____
_____

Friday _____
_{Date}

Experiences I'm Grateful For Today (Events, Opportunities, Moments, & Sensations):
_____
_____
_____

People I'm Grateful For Today (Interactions, Conversations, Kindnesses Given or Received):
_____
_____
_____

Actions & Accomplishments I'm Grateful For Today (Big & Small):
_____
_____
_____

Sources & Resources I'm Grateful For Today (Higher Power, Pets, Places, Things):
_____
_____
_____

Saturday _____
_{Date}

Experiences I'm Grateful For Today (Events, Opportunities, Moments, & Sensations):
_____
_____
_____

People I'm Grateful For Today (Interactions, Conversations, Kindnesses Given or Received):
_____
_____
_____

Actions & Accomplishments I'm Grateful For Today (Big & Small):
_____
_____
_____

Sources & Resources I'm Grateful For Today (Higher Power, Pets, Places, Things):
_____
_____
_____

Think Thankfully!
Week #14

"Thank you' is the best prayer that anyone could say. I say that one a lot. Thank you expresses extreme gratitude, humility, understanding."
~ Alice Walker

Highlights From The Research:

Hill, Allemand, & Roberts studied adults and found that an attitude of gratitude is correlated with self-reported positive physical and psychological health, as well as healthy activities and a greater willingness to seek help for health concerns.[14]

Who Will You Express Your Gratitude To This Week?

_____
_____

Sunday _____
                                    Date

Experiences I'm Grateful For Today (Events, Opportunities, Moments, & Sensations):
_____
_____
_____
_____

People I'm Grateful For Today (Interactions, Conversations, Kindnesses Given or Received):
_____
_____
_____
_____

Actions & Accomplishments I'm Grateful For Today (Big & Small):
_____
_____
_____
_____

Sources & Resources I'm Grateful For Today (Higher Power, Pets, Places, Things):
_____
_____
_____
_____

Monday _____
Date

Experiences I'm Grateful For Today (Events, Opportunities, Moments, & Sensations):
_____
_____
_____

People I'm Grateful For Today (Interactions, Conversations, Kindnesses Given or Received):
_____
_____
_____

Actions & Accomplishments I'm Grateful For Today (Big & Small):
_____
_____
_____

Sources & Resources I'm Grateful For Today (Higher Power, Pets, Places, Things):
_____
_____
_____

Tuesday _____
Date

Experiences I'm Grateful For Today (Events, Opportunities, Moments, & Sensations):
_____
_____
_____

People I'm Grateful For Today (Interactions, Conversations, Kindnesses Given or Received):
_____
_____
_____

Actions & Accomplishments I'm Grateful For Today (Big & Small):
_____
_____
_____

Sources & Resources I'm Grateful For Today (Higher Power, Pets, Places, Things):
_____
_____
_____

Wednesday _____
_{Date}

Experiences I'm Grateful For Today (Events, Opportunities, Moments, & Sensations):
_____
_____
_____

People I'm Grateful For Today (Interactions, Conversations, Kindnesses Given or Received):
_____
_____
_____
_____

Actions & Accomplishments I'm Grateful For Today (Big & Small):
_____
_____
_____
_____

Sources & Resources I'm Grateful For Today (Higher Power, Pets, Places, Things):
_____
_____
_____
_____

Thursday _____
_{Date}

Experiences I'm Grateful For Today (Events, Opportunities, Moments, & Sensations):
_____
_____
_____

People I'm Grateful For Today (Interactions, Conversations, Kindnesses Given or Received):
_____
_____
_____
_____

Actions & Accomplishments I'm Grateful For Today (Big & Small):
_____
_____
_____
_____

Sources & Resources I'm Grateful For Today (Higher Power, Pets, Places, Things):
_____
_____
_____
_____

Friday _____
Date

Experiences I'm Grateful For Today (Events, Opportunities, Moments, & Sensations):
_____
_____
_____
_____

People I'm Grateful For Today (Interactions, Conversations, Kindnesses Given or Received):
_____
_____
_____
_____

Actions & Accomplishments I'm Grateful For Today (Big & Small):
_____
_____
_____
_____

Sources & Resources I'm Grateful For Today (Higher Power, Pets, Places, Things):
_____
_____
_____
_____

Saturday _____
Date

Experiences I'm Grateful For Today (Events, Opportunities, Moments, & Sensations):
_____
_____
_____
_____

People I'm Grateful For Today (Interactions, Conversations, Kindnesses Given or Received):
_____
_____
_____
_____

Actions & Accomplishments I'm Grateful For Today (Big & Small):
_____
_____
_____
_____

Sources & Resources I'm Grateful For Today (Higher Power, Pets, Places, Things):
_____
_____
_____
_____

Think Thankfully!
Week #15

"The power of finding beauty in the humblest things makes the home happy and life lovely."
~ Louisa May Alcott

Highlights From The Research:

Chaplin, John, Rindfleisch, & Froh conducted a study of adolescents and discovered that higher levels of gratitude are correlated with lower levels of materialism.[15]

Who Will You Express Your Gratitude To This Week?

_____
_____

Sunday _____
_{Date}

Experiences I'm Grateful For Today (Events, Opportunities, Moments, & Sensations):
_____
_____
_____
_____

People I'm Grateful For Today (Interactions, Conversations, Kindnesses Given or Received):
_____
_____
_____
_____

Actions & Accomplishments I'm Grateful For Today (Big & Small):
_____
_____
_____
_____

Sources & Resources I'm Grateful For Today (Higher Power, Pets, Places, Things):
_____
_____
_____
_____

Monday _____
Date

Experiences I'm Grateful For Today (Events, Opportunities, Moments, & Sensations):
_____
_____
_____

People I'm Grateful For Today (Interactions, Conversations, Kindnesses Given or Received):
_____
_____
_____

Actions & Accomplishments I'm Grateful For Today (Big & Small):
_____
_____
_____

Sources & Resources I'm Grateful For Today (Higher Power, Pets, Places, Things):
_____
_____
_____

Tuesday _____
Date

Experiences I'm Grateful For Today (Events, Opportunities, Moments, & Sensations):
_____
_____
_____

People I'm Grateful For Today (Interactions, Conversations, Kindnesses Given or Received):
_____
_____
_____

Actions & Accomplishments I'm Grateful For Today (Big & Small):
_____
_____
_____

Sources & Resources I'm Grateful For Today (Higher Power, Pets, Places, Things):
_____
_____
_____

Wednesday _____
Date

Experiences I'm Grateful For Today (Events, Opportunities, Moments, & Sensations):
_____
_____
_____
_____

People I'm Grateful For Today (Interactions, Conversations, Kindnesses Given or Received):
_____
_____
_____
_____

Actions & Accomplishments I'm Grateful For Today (Big & Small):
_____
_____
_____
_____

Sources & Resources I'm Grateful For Today (Higher Power, Pets, Places, Things):
_____
_____
_____
_____

Thursday _____
Date

Experiences I'm Grateful For Today (Events, Opportunities, Moments, & Sensations):
_____
_____
_____
_____

People I'm Grateful For Today (Interactions, Conversations, Kindnesses Given or Received):
_____
_____
_____
_____

Actions & Accomplishments I'm Grateful For Today (Big & Small):
_____
_____
_____
_____

Sources & Resources I'm Grateful For Today (Higher Power, Pets, Places, Things):
_____
_____
_____
_____

Friday _____
Date

Experiences I'm Grateful For Today (Events, Opportunities, Moments, & Sensations):
_____
_____
_____

People I'm Grateful For Today (Interactions, Conversations, Kindnesses Given or Received):
_____
_____
_____

Actions & Accomplishments I'm Grateful For Today (Big & Small):
_____
_____
_____

Sources & Resources I'm Grateful For Today (Higher Power, Pets, Places, Things):
_____
_____
_____

Saturday _____
Date

Experiences I'm Grateful For Today (Events, Opportunities, Moments, & Sensations):
_____
_____
_____

People I'm Grateful For Today (Interactions, Conversations, Kindnesses Given or Received):
_____
_____
_____

Actions & Accomplishments I'm Grateful For Today (Big & Small):
_____
_____
_____

Sources & Resources I'm Grateful For Today (Higher Power, Pets, Places, Things):
_____
_____
_____

Think Thankfully!
Week #16

"True forgiveness is when you can say, 'Thank you for that experience.'"
~ Oprah Winfrey

Highlights From The Research:

Petrocchi conducted a study of adults and found that a grateful disposition is correlated with less depression and anxiety symptoms, less self-attacking and self-criticizing behaviors, and more self-reassuring behaviors.[16]

Who Will You Express Your Gratitude To This Week?

_____
_____

Sunday _____
Date

Experiences I'm Grateful For Today (Events, Opportunities, Moments, & Sensations):
_____
_____
_____
_____

People I'm Grateful For Today (Interactions, Conversations, Kindnesses Given or Received):
_____
_____
_____
_____

Actions & Accomplishments I'm Grateful For Today (Big & Small):
_____
_____
_____
_____

Sources & Resources I'm Grateful For Today (Higher Power, Pets, Places, Things):
_____
_____
_____
_____

Monday _____
_____Date
Experiences I'm Grateful For Today (Events, Opportunities, Moments, & Sensations):
_____
_____
_____

People I'm Grateful For Today (Interactions, Conversations, Kindnesses Given or Received):
_____
_____
_____
_____

Actions & Accomplishments I'm Grateful For Today (Big & Small):
_____
_____
_____

Sources & Resources I'm Grateful For Today (Higher Power, Pets, Places, Things):
_____
_____
_____

Tuesday _____
_____Date
Experiences I'm Grateful For Today (Events, Opportunities, Moments, & Sensations):
_____
_____
_____

People I'm Grateful For Today (Interactions, Conversations, Kindnesses Given or Received):
_____
_____
_____
_____

Actions & Accomplishments I'm Grateful For Today (Big & Small):
_____
_____
_____

Sources & Resources I'm Grateful For Today (Higher Power, Pets, Places, Things):
_____
_____
_____

Wednesday _____
Date

Experiences I'm Grateful For Today (Events, Opportunities, Moments, & Sensations):
_____
_____
_____

People I'm Grateful For Today (Interactions, Conversations, Kindnesses Given or Received):
_____
_____
_____
_____

Actions & Accomplishments I'm Grateful For Today (Big & Small):
_____
_____
_____
_____

Sources & Resources I'm Grateful For Today (Higher Power, Pets, Places, Things):
_____
_____
_____
_____

Thursday _____
Date

Experiences I'm Grateful For Today (Events, Opportunities, Moments, & Sensations):
_____
_____
_____

People I'm Grateful For Today (Interactions, Conversations, Kindnesses Given or Received):
_____
_____
_____
_____

Actions & Accomplishments I'm Grateful For Today (Big & Small):
_____
_____
_____
_____

Sources & Resources I'm Grateful For Today (Higher Power, Pets, Places, Things):
_____
_____
_____
_____

Friday _____
Date

Experiences I'm Grateful For Today (Events, Opportunities, Moments, & Sensations):
_____
_____
_____
_____

People I'm Grateful For Today (Interactions, Conversations, Kindnesses Given or Received):
_____
_____
_____
_____

Actions & Accomplishments I'm Grateful For Today (Big & Small):
_____
_____
_____
_____

Sources & Resources I'm Grateful For Today (Higher Power, Pets, Places, Things):
_____
_____
_____
_____

Saturday _____
Date

Experiences I'm Grateful For Today (Events, Opportunities, Moments, & Sensations):
_____
_____
_____
_____

People I'm Grateful For Today (Interactions, Conversations, Kindnesses Given or Received):
_____
_____
_____
_____

Actions & Accomplishments I'm Grateful For Today (Big & Small):
_____
_____
_____
_____

Sources & Resources I'm Grateful For Today (Higher Power, Pets, Places, Things):
_____
_____
_____
_____

Think Thankfully!
Week #17

"Blessed are those that can give without remembering and take without forgetting."
~ Elizabeth Bibesco

Highlights From The Research:

Lin conducted a study of college students and discovered that a grateful disposition is associated with greater self-esteem and flourishing and lower levels of depression.[17]

Who Will You Express Your Gratitude To This Week?

_____
_____

Sunday _____
_____ Date

Experiences I'm Grateful For Today (Events, Opportunities, Moments, & Sensations):
_____
_____
_____
_____

People I'm Grateful For Today (Interactions, Conversations, Kindnesses Given or Received):
_____
_____
_____
_____

Actions & Accomplishments I'm Grateful For Today (Big & Small):
_____
_____
_____
_____

Sources & Resources I'm Grateful For Today (Higher Power, Pets, Places, Things):
_____
_____
_____
_____

Monday _____
_{Date}

Experiences I'm Grateful For Today (Events, Opportunities, Moments, & Sensations):
_____
_____
_____
_____

People I'm Grateful For Today (Interactions, Conversations, Kindnesses Given or Received):
_____
_____
_____
_____

Actions & Accomplishments I'm Grateful For Today (Big & Small):
_____
_____
_____
_____

Sources & Resources I'm Grateful For Today (Higher Power, Pets, Places, Things):
_____
_____
_____
_____

Tuesday _____
_{Date}

Experiences I'm Grateful For Today (Events, Opportunities, Moments, & Sensations):
_____
_____
_____
_____

People I'm Grateful For Today (Interactions, Conversations, Kindnesses Given or Received):
_____
_____
_____
_____

Actions & Accomplishments I'm Grateful For Today (Big & Small):
_____
_____
_____
_____

Sources & Resources I'm Grateful For Today (Higher Power, Pets, Places, Things):
_____
_____
_____
_____

Wednesday _____
Date

Experiences I'm Grateful For Today (Events, Opportunities, Moments, & Sensations):
_____
_____
_____

People I'm Grateful For Today (Interactions, Conversations, Kindnesses Given or Received):
_____
_____
_____

Actions & Accomplishments I'm Grateful For Today (Big & Small):
_____
_____
_____

Sources & Resources I'm Grateful For Today (Higher Power, Pets, Places, Things):
_____
_____
_____

Thursday _____
Date

Experiences I'm Grateful For Today (Events, Opportunities, Moments, & Sensations):
_____
_____
_____

People I'm Grateful For Today (Interactions, Conversations, Kindnesses Given or Received):
_____
_____
_____

Actions & Accomplishments I'm Grateful For Today (Big & Small):
_____
_____
_____

Sources & Resources I'm Grateful For Today (Higher Power, Pets, Places, Things):
_____
_____
_____

Friday _____
Date

Experiences I'm Grateful For Today (Events, Opportunities, Moments, & Sensations):
_____
_____
_____

People I'm Grateful For Today (Interactions, Conversations, Kindnesses Given or Received):
_____
_____
_____

Actions & Accomplishments I'm Grateful For Today (Big & Small):
_____
_____
_____

Sources & Resources I'm Grateful For Today (Higher Power, Pets, Places, Things):
_____
_____
_____

Saturday _____
Date

Experiences I'm Grateful For Today (Events, Opportunities, Moments, & Sensations):
_____
_____
_____

People I'm Grateful For Today (Interactions, Conversations, Kindnesses Given or Received):
_____
_____
_____

Actions & Accomplishments I'm Grateful For Today (Big & Small):
_____
_____
_____

Sources & Resources I'm Grateful For Today (Higher Power, Pets, Places, Things):
_____
_____
_____

Think Thankfully!
Week #18

"There are only two ways to live your life. One is as though nothing is a miracle. The other is as though everything is a miracle."
~ Albert Einstein

Highlights From The Research:

Froh, Emmons, & Card conducted a study of adolescents and found that higher levels of gratitude related to higher grade point average, life satisfaction, and social engagement, as well as reduced envy and depression.[18]

Who Will You Express Your Gratitude To This Week?

_____
_____

Sunday _____
                                    Date

Experiences I'm Grateful For Today (Events, Opportunities, Moments, & Sensations):
_____
_____
_____
_____

People I'm Grateful For Today (Interactions, Conversations, Kindnesses Given or Received):
_____
_____
_____
_____

Actions & Accomplishments I'm Grateful For Today (Big & Small):
_____
_____
_____
_____

Sources & Resources I'm Grateful For Today (Higher Power, Pets, Places, Things):
_____
_____
_____
_____

Monday _____
_{Date}

Experiences I'm Grateful For Today (Events, Opportunities, Moments, & Sensations):
_____
_____
_____

People I'm Grateful For Today (Interactions, Conversations, Kindnesses Given or Received):
_____
_____
_____

Actions & Accomplishments I'm Grateful For Today (Big & Small):
_____
_____
_____

Sources & Resources I'm Grateful For Today (Higher Power, Pets, Places, Things):
_____
_____
_____

Tuesday _____
_{Date}

Experiences I'm Grateful For Today (Events, Opportunities, Moments, & Sensations):
_____
_____
_____

People I'm Grateful For Today (Interactions, Conversations, Kindnesses Given or Received):
_____
_____
_____

Actions & Accomplishments I'm Grateful For Today (Big & Small):
_____
_____
_____

Sources & Resources I'm Grateful For Today (Higher Power, Pets, Places, Things):
_____
_____
_____

Wednesday _____
_{Date}

Experiences I'm Grateful For Today (Events, Opportunities, Moments, & Sensations):
_____
_____
_____
_____

People I'm Grateful For Today (Interactions, Conversations, Kindnesses Given or Received):
_____
_____
_____
_____

Actions & Accomplishments I'm Grateful For Today (Big & Small):
_____
_____
_____
_____

Sources & Resources I'm Grateful For Today (Higher Power, Pets, Places, Things):
_____
_____
_____
_____

Thursday _____
_{Date}

Experiences I'm Grateful For Today (Events, Opportunities, Moments, & Sensations):
_____
_____
_____
_____

People I'm Grateful For Today (Interactions, Conversations, Kindnesses Given or Received):
_____
_____
_____
_____

Actions & Accomplishments I'm Grateful For Today (Big & Small):
_____
_____
_____
_____

Sources & Resources I'm Grateful For Today (Higher Power, Pets, Places, Things):
_____
_____
_____
_____

Friday _____
Date

Experiences I'm Grateful For Today (Events, Opportunities, Moments, & Sensations):
_____
_____
_____

People I'm Grateful For Today (Interactions, Conversations, Kindnesses Given or Received):
_____
_____
_____

Actions & Accomplishments I'm Grateful For Today (Big & Small):
_____
_____
_____

Sources & Resources I'm Grateful For Today (Higher Power, Pets, Places, Things):
_____
_____
_____

Saturday _____
Date

Experiences I'm Grateful For Today (Events, Opportunities, Moments, & Sensations):
_____
_____
_____

People I'm Grateful For Today (Interactions, Conversations, Kindnesses Given or Received):
_____
_____
_____

Actions & Accomplishments I'm Grateful For Today (Big & Small):
_____
_____
_____

Sources & Resources I'm Grateful For Today (Higher Power, Pets, Places, Things):
_____
_____
_____

Think Thankfully!
Week #19

*"Let us be grateful to people who make us happy.
They are the charming gardeners who make our souls blossom."
~ Marcel Proust*

Highlights From The Research:

Jackowska, Brown, Ronaldson, & Steptoe conducted a study of women who maintained a gratitude journal for two weeks. Findings showed that gratitude facilitates increased optimism and sleep quality, as well as reduced emotional distress and lower blood pressure.[19]

Who Will You Express Your Gratitude To This Week?
_____
_____

Sunday _____
_{Date}

Experiences I'm Grateful For Today (Events, Opportunities, Moments, & Sensations):
_____
_____
_____
_____

People I'm Grateful For Today (Interactions, Conversations, Kindnesses Given or Received):
_____
_____
_____
_____

Actions & Accomplishments I'm Grateful For Today (Big & Small):
_____
_____
_____
_____

Sources & Resources I'm Grateful For Today (Higher Power, Pets, Places, Things):
_____
_____
_____
_____

Monday _____
_{Date}

Experiences I'm Grateful For Today (Events, Opportunities, Moments, & Sensations):
_____
_____
_____

People I'm Grateful For Today (Interactions, Conversations, Kindnesses Given or Received):
_____
_____
_____

Actions & Accomplishments I'm Grateful For Today (Big & Small):
_____
_____
_____

Sources & Resources I'm Grateful For Today (Higher Power, Pets, Places, Things):
_____
_____
_____

Tuesday _____
_{Date}

Experiences I'm Grateful For Today (Events, Opportunities, Moments, & Sensations):
_____
_____
_____

People I'm Grateful For Today (Interactions, Conversations, Kindnesses Given or Received):
_____
_____
_____

Actions & Accomplishments I'm Grateful For Today (Big & Small):
_____
_____
_____

Sources & Resources I'm Grateful For Today (Higher Power, Pets, Places, Things):
_____
_____
_____

Wednesday _____
Date

Experiences I'm Grateful For Today (Events, Opportunities, Moments, & Sensations):
_____
_____
_____
_____

People I'm Grateful For Today (Interactions, Conversations, Kindnesses Given or Received):
_____
_____
_____
_____

Actions & Accomplishments I'm Grateful For Today (Big & Small):
_____
_____
_____
_____

Sources & Resources I'm Grateful For Today (Higher Power, Pets, Places, Things):
_____
_____
_____
_____

Thursday _____
Date

Experiences I'm Grateful For Today (Events, Opportunities, Moments, & Sensations):
_____
_____
_____
_____

People I'm Grateful For Today (Interactions, Conversations, Kindnesses Given or Received):
_____
_____
_____
_____

Actions & Accomplishments I'm Grateful For Today (Big & Small):
_____
_____
_____
_____

Sources & Resources I'm Grateful For Today (Higher Power, Pets, Places, Things):
_____
_____
_____
_____

Friday _____
<small>Date</small>

Experiences I'm Grateful For Today (Events, Opportunities, Moments, & Sensations):
_____
_____
_____

People I'm Grateful For Today (Interactions, Conversations, Kindnesses Given or Received):
_____
_____
_____

Actions & Accomplishments I'm Grateful For Today (Big & Small):
_____
_____
_____

Sources & Resources I'm Grateful For Today (Higher Power, Pets, Places, Things):
_____
_____
_____

Saturday _____
<small>Date</small>

Experiences I'm Grateful For Today (Events, Opportunities, Moments, & Sensations):
_____
_____
_____

People I'm Grateful For Today (Interactions, Conversations, Kindnesses Given or Received):
_____
_____
_____

Actions & Accomplishments I'm Grateful For Today (Big & Small):
_____
_____
_____

Sources & Resources I'm Grateful For Today (Higher Power, Pets, Places, Things):
_____
_____
_____

Think Thankfully!
Week #20

"The unthankful heart discovers no mercies; but the thankful heart will find, in every hour, some heavenly blessings."
~ Harriet Beecher Stowe

Highlights From The Research:

Chaplin, John, Rindfleisch, & Froh studied adolescents who kept a gratitude journal for two weeks and discovered that they displayed significantly reduced materialism and demonstrated more charitable behaviors.[20]

Who Will You Express Your Gratitude To This Week?
_____
_____

Sunday _____
                                    Date

Experiences I'm Grateful For Today (Events, Opportunities, Moments, & Sensations):
_____
_____
_____
_____

People I'm Grateful For Today (Interactions, Conversations, Kindnesses Given or Received):
_____
_____
_____
_____

Actions & Accomplishments I'm Grateful For Today (Big & Small):
_____
_____
_____
_____

Sources & Resources I'm Grateful For Today (Higher Power, Pets, Places, Things):
_____
_____
_____
_____

Monday _____
_{Date}

Experiences I'm Grateful For Today (Events, Opportunities, Moments, & Sensations):
_____
_____
_____

People I'm Grateful For Today (Interactions, Conversations, Kindnesses Given or Received):
_____
_____
_____

Actions & Accomplishments I'm Grateful For Today (Big & Small):
_____
_____
_____

Sources & Resources I'm Grateful For Today (Higher Power, Pets, Places, Things):
_____
_____
_____

Tuesday _____
_{Date}

Experiences I'm Grateful For Today (Events, Opportunities, Moments, & Sensations):
_____
_____
_____

People I'm Grateful For Today (Interactions, Conversations, Kindnesses Given or Received):
_____
_____
_____

Actions & Accomplishments I'm Grateful For Today (Big & Small):
_____
_____
_____

Sources & Resources I'm Grateful For Today (Higher Power, Pets, Places, Things):
_____
_____
_____

Wednesday _____
_{Date}

Experiences I'm Grateful For Today (Events, Opportunities, Moments, & Sensations):
_____
_____
_____

People I'm Grateful For Today (Interactions, Conversations, Kindnesses Given or Received):
_____
_____
_____

Actions & Accomplishments I'm Grateful For Today (Big & Small):
_____
_____
_____

Sources & Resources I'm Grateful For Today (Higher Power, Pets, Places, Things):
_____
_____
_____

Thursday _____
_{Date}

Experiences I'm Grateful For Today (Events, Opportunities, Moments, & Sensations):
_____
_____
_____

People I'm Grateful For Today (Interactions, Conversations, Kindnesses Given or Received):
_____
_____
_____

Actions & Accomplishments I'm Grateful For Today (Big & Small):
_____
_____
_____

Sources & Resources I'm Grateful For Today (Higher Power, Pets, Places, Things):
_____
_____
_____

Friday _____
Date

Experiences I'm Grateful For Today (Events, Opportunities, Moments, & Sensations):
_____
_____
_____

People I'm Grateful For Today (Interactions, Conversations, Kindnesses Given or Received):
_____
_____
_____

Actions & Accomplishments I'm Grateful For Today (Big & Small):
_____
_____
_____

Sources & Resources I'm Grateful For Today (Higher Power, Pets, Places, Things):
_____
_____
_____

Saturday _____
Date

Experiences I'm Grateful For Today (Events, Opportunities, Moments, & Sensations):
_____
_____
_____

People I'm Grateful For Today (Interactions, Conversations, Kindnesses Given or Received):
_____
_____
_____

Actions & Accomplishments I'm Grateful For Today (Big & Small):
_____
_____
_____

Sources & Resources I'm Grateful For Today (Higher Power, Pets, Places, Things):
_____
_____
_____

Think Thankfully!
Week #21

"Gratitude can transform common days into thanksgivings, turn routine jobs into joy, and change ordinary opportunities into blessings."
~ William Arthur Ward

Highlights From The Research:

Emmons & McCullough conducted a study of college students who completed a 10-week gratitude intervention, writing a list of five things they were grateful for weekly. They found that participants reported feeling better about their lives overall, more optimistic about the upcoming week, spent more time exercising, and reported fewer physical complaints.[21]

Who Will You Express Your Gratitude To This Week?

_____
_____

Sunday _____
                                              Date

Experiences I'm Grateful For Today (Events, Opportunities, Moments, & Sensations):
_____
_____
_____
_____

People I'm Grateful For Today (Interactions, Conversations, Kindnesses Given or Received):
_____
_____
_____
_____

Actions & Accomplishments I'm Grateful For Today (Big & Small):
_____
_____
_____
_____

Sources & Resources I'm Grateful For Today (Higher Power, Pets, Places, Things):
_____
_____
_____
_____

Monday _____
_{Date}

Experiences I'm Grateful For Today (Events, Opportunities, Moments, & Sensations):
_____
_____
_____
_____

People I'm Grateful For Today (Interactions, Conversations, Kindnesses Given or Received):
_____
_____
_____
_____

Actions & Accomplishments I'm Grateful For Today (Big & Small):
_____
_____
_____
_____

Sources & Resources I'm Grateful For Today (Higher Power, Pets, Places, Things):
_____
_____
_____
_____

Tuesday _____
_{Date}

Experiences I'm Grateful For Today (Events, Opportunities, Moments, & Sensations):
_____
_____
_____
_____

People I'm Grateful For Today (Interactions, Conversations, Kindnesses Given or Received):
_____
_____
_____
_____

Actions & Accomplishments I'm Grateful For Today (Big & Small):
_____
_____
_____
_____

Sources & Resources I'm Grateful For Today (Higher Power, Pets, Places, Things):
_____
_____
_____
_____

Wednesday _____
Date

Experiences I'm Grateful For Today (Events, Opportunities, Moments, & Sensations):
_____
_____
_____
_____

People I'm Grateful For Today (Interactions, Conversations, Kindnesses Given or Received):
_____
_____
_____
_____

Actions & Accomplishments I'm Grateful For Today (Big & Small):
_____
_____
_____
_____

Sources & Resources I'm Grateful For Today (Higher Power, Pets, Places, Things):
_____
_____
_____
_____

Thursday _____
Date

Experiences I'm Grateful For Today (Events, Opportunities, Moments, & Sensations):
_____
_____
_____
_____

People I'm Grateful For Today (Interactions, Conversations, Kindnesses Given or Received):
_____
_____
_____
_____

Actions & Accomplishments I'm Grateful For Today (Big & Small):
_____
_____
_____
_____

Sources & Resources I'm Grateful For Today (Higher Power, Pets, Places, Things):
_____
_____
_____
_____

Friday _____
Date

Experiences I'm Grateful For Today (Events, Opportunities, Moments, & Sensations):
_____
_____
_____

People I'm Grateful For Today (Interactions, Conversations, Kindnesses Given or Received):
_____
_____
_____

Actions & Accomplishments I'm Grateful For Today (Big & Small):
_____
_____
_____

Sources & Resources I'm Grateful For Today (Higher Power, Pets, Places, Things):
_____
_____
_____

Saturday _____
Date

Experiences I'm Grateful For Today (Events, Opportunities, Moments, & Sensations):
_____
_____
_____

People I'm Grateful For Today (Interactions, Conversations, Kindnesses Given or Received):
_____
_____
_____

Actions & Accomplishments I'm Grateful For Today (Big & Small):
_____
_____
_____

Sources & Resources I'm Grateful For Today (Higher Power, Pets, Places, Things):
_____
_____
_____

Think Thankfully!
Week #22

*"Gratitude opens the door to the power, the wisdom, the creativity of the universe.
You open the door through gratitude."*
~ Deepak Chopra

Highlights From The Research:

Killen & Macaskill studied the impact of gratitude exercises on older adults who documented three good things that occurred during the day and why they saw them as positive every evening for two weeks. The gratitude exercise was effective in decreasing stress and increasing flourishing.[22]

Who Will You Express Your Gratitude To This Week?
_____
_____

Sunday _____
                              Date

Experiences I'm Grateful For Today (Events, Opportunities, Moments, & Sensations):
_____
_____
_____
_____

People I'm Grateful For Today (Interactions, Conversations, Kindnesses Given or Received):
_____
_____
_____
_____

Actions & Accomplishments I'm Grateful For Today (Big & Small):
_____
_____
_____
_____

Sources & Resources I'm Grateful For Today (Higher Power, Pets, Places, Things):
_____
_____
_____
_____

Monday _____
Date

Experiences I'm Grateful For Today (Events, Opportunities, Moments, & Sensations):
_____
_____
_____

People I'm Grateful For Today (Interactions, Conversations, Kindnesses Given or Received):
_____
_____
_____

Actions & Accomplishments I'm Grateful For Today (Big & Small):
_____
_____
_____

Sources & Resources I'm Grateful For Today (Higher Power, Pets, Places, Things):
_____
_____
_____

Tuesday _____
Date

Experiences I'm Grateful For Today (Events, Opportunities, Moments, & Sensations):
_____
_____
_____

People I'm Grateful For Today (Interactions, Conversations, Kindnesses Given or Received):
_____
_____
_____

Actions & Accomplishments I'm Grateful For Today (Big & Small):
_____
_____
_____

Sources & Resources I'm Grateful For Today (Higher Power, Pets, Places, Things):
_____
_____
_____

Wednesday _____
_{Date}

Experiences I'm Grateful For Today (Events, Opportunities, Moments, & Sensations):
_____
_____
_____

People I'm Grateful For Today (Interactions, Conversations, Kindnesses Given or Received):
_____
_____
_____

Actions & Accomplishments I'm Grateful For Today (Big & Small):
_____
_____
_____

Sources & Resources I'm Grateful For Today (Higher Power, Pets, Places, Things):
_____
_____
_____

Thursday _____
_{Date}

Experiences I'm Grateful For Today (Events, Opportunities, Moments, & Sensations):
_____
_____
_____

People I'm Grateful For Today (Interactions, Conversations, Kindnesses Given or Received):
_____
_____
_____

Actions & Accomplishments I'm Grateful For Today (Big & Small):
_____
_____
_____

Sources & Resources I'm Grateful For Today (Higher Power, Pets, Places, Things):
_____
_____
_____

Friday _____
_{Date}

Experiences I'm Grateful For Today (Events, Opportunities, Moments, & Sensations):
_____
_____
_____

People I'm Grateful For Today (Interactions, Conversations, Kindnesses Given or Received):
_____
_____
_____

Actions & Accomplishments I'm Grateful For Today (Big & Small):
_____
_____
_____

Sources & Resources I'm Grateful For Today (Higher Power, Pets, Places, Things):
_____
_____
_____

Saturday _____
_{Date}

Experiences I'm Grateful For Today (Events, Opportunities, Moments, & Sensations):
_____
_____
_____

People I'm Grateful For Today (Interactions, Conversations, Kindnesses Given or Received):
_____
_____
_____

Actions & Accomplishments I'm Grateful For Today (Big & Small):
_____
_____
_____

Sources & Resources I'm Grateful For Today (Higher Power, Pets, Places, Things):
_____
_____
_____

Think Thankfully!
Week #23

"We learned about gratitude and humility - that so many people had a hand in our success, from the teachers who inspired us to the janitors who kept our school clean... and we were taught to value everyone's contribution and treat everyone with respect."
~ Michelle Obama

Highlights From The Research:

The John Templeton Foundation conducted a comprehensive survey on gratitude and found that 88% of people indicated that expressing gratitude to their colleagues makes them feel happier and more fulfilled.[23]

Who Will You Express Your Gratitude To This Week?

_____
_____

Sunday _____

Date

Experiences I'm Grateful For Today (Events, Opportunities, Moments, & Sensations):
_____
_____
_____
_____

People I'm Grateful For Today (Interactions, Conversations, Kindnesses Given or Received):
_____
_____
_____
_____

Actions & Accomplishments I'm Grateful For Today (Big & Small):
_____
_____
_____
_____

Sources & Resources I'm Grateful For Today (Higher Power, Pets, Places, Things):
_____
_____
_____
_____

Monday _____
_{Date}

Experiences I'm Grateful For Today (Events, Opportunities, Moments, & Sensations):
_____
_____
_____

People I'm Grateful For Today (Interactions, Conversations, Kindnesses Given or Received):
_____
_____
_____

Actions & Accomplishments I'm Grateful For Today (Big & Small):
_____
_____
_____

Sources & Resources I'm Grateful For Today (Higher Power, Pets, Places, Things):
_____
_____
_____

Tuesday _____
_{Date}

Experiences I'm Grateful For Today (Events, Opportunities, Moments, & Sensations):
_____
_____
_____

People I'm Grateful For Today (Interactions, Conversations, Kindnesses Given or Received):
_____
_____
_____

Actions & Accomplishments I'm Grateful For Today (Big & Small):
_____
_____
_____

Sources & Resources I'm Grateful For Today (Higher Power, Pets, Places, Things):
_____
_____
_____

Wednesday _____
Date

Experiences I'm Grateful For Today (Events, Opportunities, Moments, & Sensations):
_____
_____
_____
_____

People I'm Grateful For Today (Interactions, Conversations, Kindnesses Given or Received):
_____
_____
_____
_____

Actions & Accomplishments I'm Grateful For Today (Big & Small):
_____
_____
_____
_____

Sources & Resources I'm Grateful For Today (Higher Power, Pets, Places, Things):
_____
_____
_____
_____

Thursday _____
Date

Experiences I'm Grateful For Today (Events, Opportunities, Moments, & Sensations):
_____
_____
_____
_____

People I'm Grateful For Today (Interactions, Conversations, Kindnesses Given or Received):
_____
_____
_____
_____

Actions & Accomplishments I'm Grateful For Today (Big & Small):
_____
_____
_____
_____

Sources & Resources I'm Grateful For Today (Higher Power, Pets, Places, Things):
_____
_____
_____
_____

Friday _____
Date

Experiences I'm Grateful For Today (Events, Opportunities, Moments, & Sensations):
_____
_____
_____

People I'm Grateful For Today (Interactions, Conversations, Kindnesses Given or Received):
_____
_____
_____

Actions & Accomplishments I'm Grateful For Today (Big & Small):
_____
_____
_____

Sources & Resources I'm Grateful For Today (Higher Power, Pets, Places, Things):
_____
_____
_____

Saturday _____
Date

Experiences I'm Grateful For Today (Events, Opportunities, Moments, & Sensations):
_____
_____
_____

People I'm Grateful For Today (Interactions, Conversations, Kindnesses Given or Received):
_____
_____
_____

Actions & Accomplishments I'm Grateful For Today (Big & Small):
_____
_____
_____

Sources & Resources I'm Grateful For Today (Higher Power, Pets, Places, Things):
_____
_____
_____

Think Thankfully!
Week #24

"My day begins and ends with gratitude."
~ Louise Hay

Highlights From The Research:

Emmons & McCullough studied college students who completed a two-week gratitude intervention, writing a list of five things they were grateful for daily, found that participants experienced more positive emotions and were more likely to help someone with a personal problem or offer someone emotional support.[24]

Who Will You Express Your Gratitude To This Week?

_____
_____

Sunday _____
                                            Date

Experiences I'm Grateful For Today (Events, Opportunities, Moments, & Sensations):
_____
_____
_____
_____

People I'm Grateful For Today (Interactions, Conversations, Kindnesses Given or Received):
_____
_____
_____
_____

Actions & Accomplishments I'm Grateful For Today (Big & Small):
_____
_____
_____
_____

Sources & Resources I'm Grateful For Today (Higher Power, Pets, Places, Things):
_____
_____
_____
_____

Monday _____
_{Date}

Experiences I'm Grateful For Today (Events, Opportunities, Moments, & Sensations):
_____
_____
_____

People I'm Grateful For Today (Interactions, Conversations, Kindnesses Given or Received):
_____
_____
_____

Actions & Accomplishments I'm Grateful For Today (Big & Small):
_____
_____
_____

Sources & Resources I'm Grateful For Today (Higher Power, Pets, Places, Things):
_____
_____
_____

Tuesday _____
_{Date}

Experiences I'm Grateful For Today (Events, Opportunities, Moments, & Sensations):
_____
_____
_____

People I'm Grateful For Today (Interactions, Conversations, Kindnesses Given or Received):
_____
_____
_____

Actions & Accomplishments I'm Grateful For Today (Big & Small):
_____
_____
_____

Sources & Resources I'm Grateful For Today (Higher Power, Pets, Places, Things):
_____
_____
_____

Wednesday _____
Date

Experiences I'm Grateful For Today (Events, Opportunities, Moments, & Sensations):
_____
_____
_____

People I'm Grateful For Today (Interactions, Conversations, Kindnesses Given or Received):
_____
_____
_____

Actions & Accomplishments I'm Grateful For Today (Big & Small):
_____
_____
_____

Sources & Resources I'm Grateful For Today (Higher Power, Pets, Places, Things):
_____
_____
_____

Thursday _____
Date

Experiences I'm Grateful For Today (Events, Opportunities, Moments, & Sensations):
_____
_____
_____

People I'm Grateful For Today (Interactions, Conversations, Kindnesses Given or Received):
_____
_____
_____

Actions & Accomplishments I'm Grateful For Today (Big & Small):
_____
_____
_____

Sources & Resources I'm Grateful For Today (Higher Power, Pets, Places, Things):
_____
_____
_____

Friday _____
Date

Experiences I'm Grateful For Today (Events, Opportunities, Moments, & Sensations):
_____
_____
_____

People I'm Grateful For Today (Interactions, Conversations, Kindnesses Given or Received):
_____
_____
_____

Actions & Accomplishments I'm Grateful For Today (Big & Small):
_____
_____
_____

Sources & Resources I'm Grateful For Today (Higher Power, Pets, Places, Things):
_____
_____
_____

Saturday _____
Date

Experiences I'm Grateful For Today (Events, Opportunities, Moments, & Sensations):
_____
_____
_____

People I'm Grateful For Today (Interactions, Conversations, Kindnesses Given or Received):
_____
_____
_____

Actions & Accomplishments I'm Grateful For Today (Big & Small):
_____
_____
_____

Sources & Resources I'm Grateful For Today (Higher Power, Pets, Places, Things):
_____
_____
_____

Think Thankfully!
Week #25

"The more grateful I am, the more beauty I see."
~ Mary Davis

Highlights From The Research:

Michie studied managers and employees from different organizations in a variety of industries, including financial services, consulting, health care, construction, manufacturing, and retail sales, and discovered that leaders with higher levels of gratitude are more likely to recognize their employees' contributions and treat them with dignity and respect.[25]

Who Will You Express Your Gratitude To This Week?

_____
_____

Sunday _____
Date

Experiences I'm Grateful For Today (Events, Opportunities, Moments, & Sensations):
_____
_____
_____
_____

People I'm Grateful For Today (Interactions, Conversations, Kindnesses Given or Received):
_____
_____
_____
_____

Actions & Accomplishments I'm Grateful For Today (Big & Small):
_____
_____
_____
_____

Sources & Resources I'm Grateful For Today (Higher Power, Pets, Places, Things):
_____
_____
_____
_____

Monday _____
_{Date}

Experiences I'm Grateful For Today (Events, Opportunities, Moments, & Sensations):
_____
_____
_____

People I'm Grateful For Today (Interactions, Conversations, Kindnesses Given or Received):
_____
_____
_____

Actions & Accomplishments I'm Grateful For Today (Big & Small):
_____
_____
_____

Sources & Resources I'm Grateful For Today (Higher Power, Pets, Places, Things):
_____
_____
_____

Tuesday _____
_{Date}

Experiences I'm Grateful For Today (Events, Opportunities, Moments, & Sensations):
_____
_____
_____

People I'm Grateful For Today (Interactions, Conversations, Kindnesses Given or Received):
_____
_____
_____

Actions & Accomplishments I'm Grateful For Today (Big & Small):
_____
_____
_____

Sources & Resources I'm Grateful For Today (Higher Power, Pets, Places, Things):
_____
_____
_____

Wednesday _____
_{Date}

Experiences I'm Grateful For Today (Events, Opportunities, Moments, & Sensations):
_____
_____
_____

People I'm Grateful For Today (Interactions, Conversations, Kindnesses Given or Received):
_____
_____
_____

Actions & Accomplishments I'm Grateful For Today (Big & Small):
_____
_____
_____

Sources & Resources I'm Grateful For Today (Higher Power, Pets, Places, Things):
_____
_____
_____

Thursday _____
_{Date}

Experiences I'm Grateful For Today (Events, Opportunities, Moments, & Sensations):
_____
_____
_____

People I'm Grateful For Today (Interactions, Conversations, Kindnesses Given or Received):
_____
_____
_____

Actions & Accomplishments I'm Grateful For Today (Big & Small):
_____
_____
_____

Sources & Resources I'm Grateful For Today (Higher Power, Pets, Places, Things):
_____
_____
_____

Friday _____
Date

Experiences I'm Grateful For Today (Events, Opportunities, Moments, & Sensations):
_____
_____
_____

People I'm Grateful For Today (Interactions, Conversations, Kindnesses Given or Received):
_____
_____
_____

Actions & Accomplishments I'm Grateful For Today (Big & Small):
_____
_____
_____

Sources & Resources I'm Grateful For Today (Higher Power, Pets, Places, Things):
_____
_____
_____

Saturday _____
Date

Experiences I'm Grateful For Today (Events, Opportunities, Moments, & Sensations):
_____
_____
_____

People I'm Grateful For Today (Interactions, Conversations, Kindnesses Given or Received):
_____
_____
_____

Actions & Accomplishments I'm Grateful For Today (Big & Small):
_____
_____
_____

Sources & Resources I'm Grateful For Today (Higher Power, Pets, Places, Things):
_____
_____
_____

Think Thankfully!
Week #26

"The struggle ends when gratitude begins."
~ Neale Donald Walsch

Highlights From The Research:

Wong, Owen, Gabana, Brown, McInnis, Toth, & Gilman conducted a study of college students who participated in three sessions over three weeks, writing letters of gratitude to a person they had not properly thanked, describing what the person did for them, how they impacted their lives, and how they felt toward them. Participants reported better mental health than counterparts who did not write gratitude letters.[26]

Who Will You Express Your Gratitude To This Week?

_____

Sunday _____
                                 Date

Experiences I'm Grateful For Today (Events, Opportunities, Moments, & Sensations):
_____
_____
_____
_____

People I'm Grateful For Today (Interactions, Conversations, Kindnesses Given or Received):
_____
_____
_____
_____

Actions & Accomplishments I'm Grateful For Today (Big & Small):
_____
_____
_____
_____

Sources & Resources I'm Grateful For Today (Higher Power, Pets, Places, Things):
_____
_____
_____
_____

Monday _____
_{Date}

Experiences I'm Grateful For Today (Events, Opportunities, Moments, & Sensations):
_____
_____
_____
_____

People I'm Grateful For Today (Interactions, Conversations, Kindnesses Given or Received):
_____
_____
_____
_____

Actions & Accomplishments I'm Grateful For Today (Big & Small):
_____
_____
_____
_____

Sources & Resources I'm Grateful For Today (Higher Power, Pets, Places, Things):
_____
_____
_____
_____

Tuesday _____
_{Date}

Experiences I'm Grateful For Today (Events, Opportunities, Moments, & Sensations):
_____
_____
_____
_____

People I'm Grateful For Today (Interactions, Conversations, Kindnesses Given or Received):
_____
_____
_____
_____

Actions & Accomplishments I'm Grateful For Today (Big & Small):
_____
_____
_____
_____

Sources & Resources I'm Grateful For Today (Higher Power, Pets, Places, Things):
_____
_____
_____
_____

Wednesday _____
_{Date}

Experiences I'm Grateful For Today (Events, Opportunities, Moments, & Sensations):
_____
_____
_____
_____

People I'm Grateful For Today (Interactions, Conversations, Kindnesses Given or Received):
_____
_____
_____
_____

Actions & Accomplishments I'm Grateful For Today (Big & Small):
_____
_____
_____
_____

Sources & Resources I'm Grateful For Today (Higher Power, Pets, Places, Things):
_____
_____
_____
_____

Thursday _____
_{Date}

Experiences I'm Grateful For Today (Events, Opportunities, Moments, & Sensations):
_____
_____
_____
_____

People I'm Grateful For Today (Interactions, Conversations, Kindnesses Given or Received):
_____
_____
_____
_____

Actions & Accomplishments I'm Grateful For Today (Big & Small):
_____
_____
_____
_____

Sources & Resources I'm Grateful For Today (Higher Power, Pets, Places, Things):
_____
_____
_____
_____

Friday _____
Date

Experiences I'm Grateful For Today (Events, Opportunities, Moments, & Sensations):
_____
_____
_____

People I'm Grateful For Today (Interactions, Conversations, Kindnesses Given or Received):
_____
_____
_____

Actions & Accomplishments I'm Grateful For Today (Big & Small):
_____
_____
_____

Sources & Resources I'm Grateful For Today (Higher Power, Pets, Places, Things):
_____
_____
_____

Saturday _____
Date

Experiences I'm Grateful For Today (Events, Opportunities, Moments, & Sensations):
_____
_____
_____

People I'm Grateful For Today (Interactions, Conversations, Kindnesses Given or Received):
_____
_____
_____

Actions & Accomplishments I'm Grateful For Today (Big & Small):
_____
_____
_____

Sources & Resources I'm Grateful For Today (Higher Power, Pets, Places, Things):
_____
_____
_____

Think Thankfully!
Week #27

"The roots of all goodness lie in the soil of appreciation for goodness."
~ Dalai Lama

Highlights From The Research:

Burke, Ng, & Fiksenbaum studied nurses and found that those scoring higher on gratitude indicated greater job satisfaction, life satisfaction, vigor, dedication, and efficacy; less work absences, exhaustion, psychosomatic symptoms, and cynicism; and higher ratings of their work health/safety climate and quality of health care at work; and perceiving higher levels of hospital support.[27]

Who Will You Express Your Gratitude To This Week?

_____
_____

Sunday _____
                                    Date

Experiences I'm Grateful For Today (Events, Opportunities, Moments, & Sensations):
_____
_____
_____
_____

People I'm Grateful For Today (Interactions, Conversations, Kindnesses Given or Received):
_____
_____
_____
_____

Actions & Accomplishments I'm Grateful For Today (Big & Small):
_____
_____
_____
_____

Sources & Resources I'm Grateful For Today (Higher Power, Pets, Places, Things):
_____
_____
_____
_____

Monday _____
Date

Experiences I'm Grateful For Today (Events, Opportunities, Moments, & Sensations):
_____
_____
_____
_____

People I'm Grateful For Today (Interactions, Conversations, Kindnesses Given or Received):
_____
_____
_____
_____

Actions & Accomplishments I'm Grateful For Today (Big & Small):
_____
_____
_____
_____

Sources & Resources I'm Grateful For Today (Higher Power, Pets, Places, Things):
_____
_____
_____
_____

Tuesday _____
Date

Experiences I'm Grateful For Today (Events, Opportunities, Moments, & Sensations):
_____
_____
_____
_____

People I'm Grateful For Today (Interactions, Conversations, Kindnesses Given or Received):
_____
_____
_____
_____

Actions & Accomplishments I'm Grateful For Today (Big & Small):
_____
_____
_____
_____

Sources & Resources I'm Grateful For Today (Higher Power, Pets, Places, Things):
_____
_____
_____
_____

Wednesday _____
_{Date}

Experiences I'm Grateful For Today (Events, Opportunities, Moments, & Sensations):
_____
_____
_____
_____

People I'm Grateful For Today (Interactions, Conversations, Kindnesses Given or Received):
_____
_____
_____
_____

Actions & Accomplishments I'm Grateful For Today (Big & Small):
_____
_____
_____
_____

Sources & Resources I'm Grateful For Today (Higher Power, Pets, Places, Things):
_____
_____
_____
_____

Thursday _____
_{Date}

Experiences I'm Grateful For Today (Events, Opportunities, Moments, & Sensations):
_____
_____
_____
_____

People I'm Grateful For Today (Interactions, Conversations, Kindnesses Given or Received):
_____
_____
_____
_____

Actions & Accomplishments I'm Grateful For Today (Big & Small):
_____
_____
_____
_____

Sources & Resources I'm Grateful For Today (Higher Power, Pets, Places, Things):
_____
_____
_____
_____

Friday _____
_{Date}

Experiences I'm Grateful For Today (Events, Opportunities, Moments, & Sensations):
_____
_____
_____
_____

People I'm Grateful For Today (Interactions, Conversations, Kindnesses Given or Received):
_____
_____
_____
_____

Actions & Accomplishments I'm Grateful For Today (Big & Small):
_____
_____
_____
_____

Sources & Resources I'm Grateful For Today (Higher Power, Pets, Places, Things):
_____
_____
_____
_____

Saturday _____
_{Date}

Experiences I'm Grateful For Today (Events, Opportunities, Moments, & Sensations):
_____
_____
_____
_____

People I'm Grateful For Today (Interactions, Conversations, Kindnesses Given or Received):
_____
_____
_____
_____

Actions & Accomplishments I'm Grateful For Today (Big & Small):
_____
_____
_____
_____

Sources & Resources I'm Grateful For Today (Higher Power, Pets, Places, Things):
_____
_____
_____
_____

Think Thankfully!
Week #28

"There are always flowers for those who want to see them."
~ Henri Matisse

Highlights From The Research:

Hoy, Suldo, & Raffaele Mendez studied levels of gratitude and life satisfaction of parents and children and found a significant relationship between mother and child gratitude, as well as child life satisfaction and both mothers' and fathers' life satisfaction.[28]

Who Will You Express Your Gratitude To This Week?
_____
_____

Sunday _____
                                        Date

Experiences I'm Grateful For Today (Events, Opportunities, Moments, & Sensations):
_____
_____
_____
_____

People I'm Grateful For Today (Interactions, Conversations, Kindnesses Given or Received):
_____
_____
_____
_____

Actions & Accomplishments I'm Grateful For Today (Big & Small):
_____
_____
_____
_____

Sources & Resources I'm Grateful For Today (Higher Power, Pets, Places, Things):
_____
_____
_____
_____

Monday _____
_{Date}

Experiences I'm Grateful For Today (Events, Opportunities, Moments, & Sensations):
_____
_____
_____

People I'm Grateful For Today (Interactions, Conversations, Kindnesses Given or Received):
_____
_____
_____

Actions & Accomplishments I'm Grateful For Today (Big & Small):
_____
_____
_____

Sources & Resources I'm Grateful For Today (Higher Power, Pets, Places, Things):
_____
_____
_____

Tuesday _____
_{Date}

Experiences I'm Grateful For Today (Events, Opportunities, Moments, & Sensations):
_____
_____
_____

People I'm Grateful For Today (Interactions, Conversations, Kindnesses Given or Received):
_____
_____
_____

Actions & Accomplishments I'm Grateful For Today (Big & Small):
_____
_____
_____

Sources & Resources I'm Grateful For Today (Higher Power, Pets, Places, Things):
_____
_____
_____

Wednesday _____
Date

Experiences I'm Grateful For Today (Events, Opportunities, Moments, & Sensations):
_____
_____
_____

People I'm Grateful For Today (Interactions, Conversations, Kindnesses Given or Received):
_____
_____
_____

Actions & Accomplishments I'm Grateful For Today (Big & Small):
_____
_____
_____

Sources & Resources I'm Grateful For Today (Higher Power, Pets, Places, Things):
_____
_____
_____

Thursday _____
Date

Experiences I'm Grateful For Today (Events, Opportunities, Moments, & Sensations):
_____
_____
_____

People I'm Grateful For Today (Interactions, Conversations, Kindnesses Given or Received):
_____
_____
_____

Actions & Accomplishments I'm Grateful For Today (Big & Small):
_____
_____
_____

Sources & Resources I'm Grateful For Today (Higher Power, Pets, Places, Things):
_____
_____
_____

Friday _____
Date

Experiences I'm Grateful For Today (Events, Opportunities, Moments, & Sensations):
_____
_____
_____

People I'm Grateful For Today (Interactions, Conversations, Kindnesses Given or Received):
_____
_____
_____

Actions & Accomplishments I'm Grateful For Today (Big & Small):
_____
_____
_____

Sources & Resources I'm Grateful For Today (Higher Power, Pets, Places, Things):
_____
_____
_____

Saturday _____
Date

Experiences I'm Grateful For Today (Events, Opportunities, Moments, & Sensations):
_____
_____
_____

People I'm Grateful For Today (Interactions, Conversations, Kindnesses Given or Received):
_____
_____
_____

Actions & Accomplishments I'm Grateful For Today (Big & Small):
_____
_____
_____

Sources & Resources I'm Grateful For Today (Higher Power, Pets, Places, Things):
_____
_____
_____

Think Thankfully!
Week #29

"This a wonderful day. I've never seen this one before."
~ Maya Angelou

Highlights From The Research:

Howells conducted a year-long, organizationally-based gratitude intervention with teachers from two schools. Teachers formed a gratitude group and met each week in the staff room to explore gratitude. Study results indicated that teachers in the gratitude group reported improved well-being and relationships.[29]

Who Will You Express Your Gratitude To This Week?

_____
_____

Sunday _____
                              Date

Experiences I'm Grateful For Today (Events, Opportunities, Moments, & Sensations):
_____
_____
_____
_____

People I'm Grateful For Today (Interactions, Conversations, Kindnesses Given or Received):
_____
_____
_____
_____

Actions & Accomplishments I'm Grateful For Today (Big & Small):
_____
_____
_____
_____

Sources & Resources I'm Grateful For Today (Higher Power, Pets, Places, Things):
_____
_____
_____
_____

Monday _____
                                    Date
Experiences I'm Grateful For Today (Events, Opportunities, Moments, & Sensations):
_____
_____
_____

People I'm Grateful For Today (Interactions, Conversations, Kindnesses Given or Received):
_____
_____
_____

Actions & Accomplishments I'm Grateful For Today (Big & Small):
_____
_____
_____

Sources & Resources I'm Grateful For Today (Higher Power, Pets, Places, Things):
_____
_____
_____

Tuesday _____
                                    Date
Experiences I'm Grateful For Today (Events, Opportunities, Moments, & Sensations):
_____
_____
_____

People I'm Grateful For Today (Interactions, Conversations, Kindnesses Given or Received):
_____
_____
_____

Actions & Accomplishments I'm Grateful For Today (Big & Small):
_____
_____
_____

Sources & Resources I'm Grateful For Today (Higher Power, Pets, Places, Things):
_____
_____
_____

Wednesday _____
Date

Experiences I'm Grateful For Today (Events, Opportunities, Moments, & Sensations):
_____
_____
_____

People I'm Grateful For Today (Interactions, Conversations, Kindnesses Given or Received):
_____
_____
_____

Actions & Accomplishments I'm Grateful For Today (Big & Small):
_____
_____
_____

Sources & Resources I'm Grateful For Today (Higher Power, Pets, Places, Things):
_____
_____
_____

Thursday _____
Date

Experiences I'm Grateful For Today (Events, Opportunities, Moments, & Sensations):
_____
_____
_____

People I'm Grateful For Today (Interactions, Conversations, Kindnesses Given or Received):
_____
_____
_____

Actions & Accomplishments I'm Grateful For Today (Big & Small):
_____
_____
_____

Sources & Resources I'm Grateful For Today (Higher Power, Pets, Places, Things):
_____
_____
_____

Friday _____
_____Date_____

Experiences I'm Grateful For Today (Events, Opportunities, Moments, & Sensations):
_____
_____
_____

People I'm Grateful For Today (Interactions, Conversations, Kindnesses Given or Received):
_____
_____
_____

Actions & Accomplishments I'm Grateful For Today (Big & Small):
_____
_____
_____

Sources & Resources I'm Grateful For Today (Higher Power, Pets, Places, Things):
_____
_____
_____

Saturday _____
_____Date_____

Experiences I'm Grateful For Today (Events, Opportunities, Moments, & Sensations):
_____
_____
_____

People I'm Grateful For Today (Interactions, Conversations, Kindnesses Given or Received):
_____
_____
_____

Actions & Accomplishments I'm Grateful For Today (Big & Small):
_____
_____
_____

Sources & Resources I'm Grateful For Today (Higher Power, Pets, Places, Things):
_____
_____
_____

Think Thankfully!
Week #30

"As a child, I didn't know what I didn't have. I'm thankful for the challenges early on in my life because now I have a perspective on the world and kind of know what's important."
~ America Ferrera

Highlights From The Research:

Algoe, Gable, & Maisel studied couples and found that a partner's thoughtful gesture on one day enhanced feelings of gratitude and indebtedness, as well as increased feelings of relationship quality. Gratitude felt on the previous day also correlated with women's feelings of enhanced satisfaction with the relationship and men's feelings of enhanced connection with their partner and satisfaction with the relationship. Furthermore, men and women with grateful partners felt greater connection with their partner and more satisfaction with their romantic relationship than they had the previous day.[30]

Who Will You Express Your Gratitude To This Week?

_____
_____

Sunday _____
                              Date

Experiences I'm Grateful For Today (Events, Opportunities, Moments, & Sensations):
_____
_____
_____
_____

People I'm Grateful For Today (Interactions, Conversations, Kindnesses Given or Received):
_____
_____
_____
_____

Actions & Accomplishments I'm Grateful For Today (Big & Small):
_____
_____
_____
_____

Sources & Resources I'm Grateful For Today (Higher Power, Pets, Places, Things):
_____
_____
_____
_____

Monday _____
_____ Date

Experiences I'm Grateful For Today (Events, Opportunities, Moments, & Sensations):
_____
_____
_____

People I'm Grateful For Today (Interactions, Conversations, Kindnesses Given or Received):
_____
_____
_____

Actions & Accomplishments I'm Grateful For Today (Big & Small):
_____
_____
_____

Sources & Resources I'm Grateful For Today (Higher Power, Pets, Places, Things):
_____
_____
_____

Tuesday _____
_____ Date

Experiences I'm Grateful For Today (Events, Opportunities, Moments, & Sensations):
_____
_____
_____

People I'm Grateful For Today (Interactions, Conversations, Kindnesses Given or Received):
_____
_____
_____

Actions & Accomplishments I'm Grateful For Today (Big & Small):
_____
_____
_____

Sources & Resources I'm Grateful For Today (Higher Power, Pets, Places, Things):
_____
_____
_____

Wednesday _____
Date

Experiences I'm Grateful For Today (Events, Opportunities, Moments, & Sensations):
_____
_____
_____
_____

People I'm Grateful For Today (Interactions, Conversations, Kindnesses Given or Received):
_____
_____
_____
_____

Actions & Accomplishments I'm Grateful For Today (Big & Small):
_____
_____
_____
_____

Sources & Resources I'm Grateful For Today (Higher Power, Pets, Places, Things):
_____
_____
_____
_____

Thursday _____
Date

Experiences I'm Grateful For Today (Events, Opportunities, Moments, & Sensations):
_____
_____
_____
_____

People I'm Grateful For Today (Interactions, Conversations, Kindnesses Given or Received):
_____
_____
_____
_____

Actions & Accomplishments I'm Grateful For Today (Big & Small):
_____
_____
_____
_____

Sources & Resources I'm Grateful For Today (Higher Power, Pets, Places, Things):
_____
_____
_____
_____

Friday _____
_{Date}

Experiences I'm Grateful For Today (Events, Opportunities, Moments, & Sensations):
_____
_____
_____
_____

People I'm Grateful For Today (Interactions, Conversations, Kindnesses Given or Received):
_____
_____
_____
_____

Actions & Accomplishments I'm Grateful For Today (Big & Small):
_____
_____
_____
_____

Sources & Resources I'm Grateful For Today (Higher Power, Pets, Places, Things):
_____
_____
_____
_____

Saturday _____
_{Date}

Experiences I'm Grateful For Today (Events, Opportunities, Moments, & Sensations):
_____
_____
_____
_____

People I'm Grateful For Today (Interactions, Conversations, Kindnesses Given or Received):
_____
_____
_____
_____

Actions & Accomplishments I'm Grateful For Today (Big & Small):
_____
_____
_____
_____

Sources & Resources I'm Grateful For Today (Higher Power, Pets, Places, Things):
_____
_____
_____
_____

Think Thankfully!
Week #31

"Make it a habit to tell people thank you. To express your appreciation, sincerely and without the expectation of anything in return. Truly appreciate those around you, and you'll soon find many others around you."
~ Ralph Marston

Highlights From The Research:

Waters conducted a study of employees across two different industries, teaching and finance, assessing the impact of employee perceptions of gratitude on job satisfaction. Waters found that institutionalized gratitude—gratitude embedded within an organization, through its people, policies, and practices—significantly predicted employees' job satisfaction.[31]

Who Will You Express Your Gratitude To This Week?

_____
_____

Sunday _____
_____Date_____

Experiences I'm Grateful For Today (Events, Opportunities, Moments, & Sensations):
_____
_____
_____
_____

People I'm Grateful For Today (Interactions, Conversations, Kindnesses Given or Received):
_____
_____
_____
_____

Actions & Accomplishments I'm Grateful For Today (Big & Small):
_____
_____
_____
_____

Sources & Resources I'm Grateful For Today (Higher Power, Pets, Places, Things):
_____
_____
_____
_____

Monday _____
_{Date}

Experiences I'm Grateful For Today (Events, Opportunities, Moments, & Sensations):
_____
_____
_____

People I'm Grateful For Today (Interactions, Conversations, Kindnesses Given or Received):
_____
_____
_____
_____

Actions & Accomplishments I'm Grateful For Today (Big & Small):
_____
_____
_____
_____

Sources & Resources I'm Grateful For Today (Higher Power, Pets, Places, Things):
_____
_____
_____
_____

Tuesday _____
_{Date}

Experiences I'm Grateful For Today (Events, Opportunities, Moments, & Sensations):
_____
_____
_____

People I'm Grateful For Today (Interactions, Conversations, Kindnesses Given or Received):
_____
_____
_____
_____

Actions & Accomplishments I'm Grateful For Today (Big & Small):
_____
_____
_____
_____

Sources & Resources I'm Grateful For Today (Higher Power, Pets, Places, Things):
_____
_____
_____
_____

Wednesday _____
_{Date}

Experiences I'm Grateful For Today (Events, Opportunities, Moments, & Sensations):
_____
_____
_____
_____

People I'm Grateful For Today (Interactions, Conversations, Kindnesses Given or Received):
_____
_____
_____
_____

Actions & Accomplishments I'm Grateful For Today (Big & Small):
_____
_____
_____
_____

Sources & Resources I'm Grateful For Today (Higher Power, Pets, Places, Things):
_____
_____
_____
_____

Thursday _____
_{Date}

Experiences I'm Grateful For Today (Events, Opportunities, Moments, & Sensations):
_____
_____
_____
_____

People I'm Grateful For Today (Interactions, Conversations, Kindnesses Given or Received):
_____
_____
_____
_____

Actions & Accomplishments I'm Grateful For Today (Big & Small):
_____
_____
_____
_____

Sources & Resources I'm Grateful For Today (Higher Power, Pets, Places, Things):
_____
_____
_____
_____

Friday _____
Date

Experiences I'm Grateful For Today (Events, Opportunities, Moments, & Sensations):
_____
_____
_____

People I'm Grateful For Today (Interactions, Conversations, Kindnesses Given or Received):
_____
_____
_____

Actions & Accomplishments I'm Grateful For Today (Big & Small):
_____
_____
_____

Sources & Resources I'm Grateful For Today (Higher Power, Pets, Places, Things):
_____
_____
_____

Saturday _____
Date

Experiences I'm Grateful For Today (Events, Opportunities, Moments, & Sensations):
_____
_____
_____

People I'm Grateful For Today (Interactions, Conversations, Kindnesses Given or Received):
_____
_____
_____

Actions & Accomplishments I'm Grateful For Today (Big & Small):
_____
_____
_____

Sources & Resources I'm Grateful For Today (Higher Power, Pets, Places, Things):
_____
_____
_____

Think Thankfully!
Week #32

"When we give cheerfully and accept gratefully, everyone is blessed."
~ Maya Angelou

Highlights From The Research:

Froh, Kashdan, Ozimkowski, & Miller studied gratitude in children and adolescents. Participants wrote a letter to someone they were grateful for, read the letter to the person, and shared their experience with others. Participants reported greater gratitude and positive emotions after the gratitude intervention.[32]

Who Will You Express Your Gratitude To This Week?

_____
_____

Sunday _____
                              Date

Experiences I'm Grateful For Today (Events, Opportunities, Moments, & Sensations):
_____
_____
_____
_____

People I'm Grateful For Today (Interactions, Conversations, Kindnesses Given or Received):
_____
_____
_____
_____

Actions & Accomplishments I'm Grateful For Today (Big & Small):
_____
_____
_____
_____

Sources & Resources I'm Grateful For Today (Higher Power, Pets, Places, Things):
_____
_____
_____
_____

Monday _____
_{Date}

Experiences I'm Grateful For Today (Events, Opportunities, Moments, & Sensations):
_____
_____
_____

People I'm Grateful For Today (Interactions, Conversations, Kindnesses Given or Received):
_____
_____
_____

Actions & Accomplishments I'm Grateful For Today (Big & Small):
_____
_____
_____

Sources & Resources I'm Grateful For Today (Higher Power, Pets, Places, Things):
_____
_____
_____

Tuesday _____
_{Date}

Experiences I'm Grateful For Today (Events, Opportunities, Moments, & Sensations):
_____
_____
_____

People I'm Grateful For Today (Interactions, Conversations, Kindnesses Given or Received):
_____
_____
_____

Actions & Accomplishments I'm Grateful For Today (Big & Small):
_____
_____
_____

Sources & Resources I'm Grateful For Today (Higher Power, Pets, Places, Things):
_____
_____
_____

Wednesday _____
Date

Experiences I'm Grateful For Today (Events, Opportunities, Moments, & Sensations):
_____
_____
_____

People I'm Grateful For Today (Interactions, Conversations, Kindnesses Given or Received):
_____
_____
_____
_____

Actions & Accomplishments I'm Grateful For Today (Big & Small):
_____
_____
_____
_____

Sources & Resources I'm Grateful For Today (Higher Power, Pets, Places, Things):
_____
_____
_____
_____

Thursday _____
Date

Experiences I'm Grateful For Today (Events, Opportunities, Moments, & Sensations):
_____
_____
_____

People I'm Grateful For Today (Interactions, Conversations, Kindnesses Given or Received):
_____
_____
_____
_____

Actions & Accomplishments I'm Grateful For Today (Big & Small):
_____
_____
_____
_____

Sources & Resources I'm Grateful For Today (Higher Power, Pets, Places, Things):
_____
_____
_____
_____

Friday _____
Date

Experiences I'm Grateful For Today (Events, Opportunities, Moments, & Sensations):
_____
_____
_____

People I'm Grateful For Today (Interactions, Conversations, Kindnesses Given or Received):
_____
_____
_____

Actions & Accomplishments I'm Grateful For Today (Big & Small):
_____
_____
_____

Sources & Resources I'm Grateful For Today (Higher Power, Pets, Places, Things):
_____
_____
_____

Saturday _____
Date

Experiences I'm Grateful For Today (Events, Opportunities, Moments, & Sensations):
_____
_____
_____

People I'm Grateful For Today (Interactions, Conversations, Kindnesses Given or Received):
_____
_____
_____

Actions & Accomplishments I'm Grateful For Today (Big & Small):
_____
_____
_____

Sources & Resources I'm Grateful For Today (Higher Power, Pets, Places, Things):
_____
_____
_____

Think Thankfully!
Week #33

"Wear gratitude like a cloak, and it will feed every corner of your life."
~ Rumi

Highlights From The Research:

Andersson, Giacalone, & Jurkierwics conducted a study of managers and found that stronger feelings of gratitude increase leaders' concern for corporate social responsibility, facilitating their sense of accountability toward employees and philanthropy in the larger community.[33]

Who Will You Express Your Gratitude To This Week?
_____
_____

Sunday _____
                              Date

Experiences I'm Grateful For Today (Events, Opportunities, Moments, & Sensations):
_____
_____
_____
_____

People I'm Grateful For Today (Interactions, Conversations, Kindnesses Given or Received):
_____
_____
_____
_____

Actions & Accomplishments I'm Grateful For Today (Big & Small):
_____
_____
_____
_____

Sources & Resources I'm Grateful For Today (Higher Power, Pets, Places, Things):
_____
_____
_____
_____

Monday _____
_{Date}

Experiences I'm Grateful For Today (Events, Opportunities, Moments, & Sensations):
_____
_____
_____

People I'm Grateful For Today (Interactions, Conversations, Kindnesses Given or Received):
_____
_____
_____

Actions & Accomplishments I'm Grateful For Today (Big & Small):
_____
_____
_____

Sources & Resources I'm Grateful For Today (Higher Power, Pets, Places, Things):
_____
_____

Tuesday _____
_{Date}

Experiences I'm Grateful For Today (Events, Opportunities, Moments, & Sensations):
_____
_____
_____

People I'm Grateful For Today (Interactions, Conversations, Kindnesses Given or Received):
_____
_____
_____

Actions & Accomplishments I'm Grateful For Today (Big & Small):
_____
_____
_____

Sources & Resources I'm Grateful For Today (Higher Power, Pets, Places, Things):
_____
_____

Wednesday _____
                                  Date
Experiences I'm Grateful For Today (Events, Opportunities, Moments, & Sensations):
_____
_____
_____
_____

People I'm Grateful For Today (Interactions, Conversations, Kindnesses Given or Received):
_____
_____
_____
_____

Actions & Accomplishments I'm Grateful For Today (Big & Small):
_____
_____
_____
_____

Sources & Resources I'm Grateful For Today (Higher Power, Pets, Places, Things):
_____
_____
_____
_____

Thursday _____
                                  Date
Experiences I'm Grateful For Today (Events, Opportunities, Moments, & Sensations):
_____
_____
_____
_____

People I'm Grateful For Today (Interactions, Conversations, Kindnesses Given or Received):
_____
_____
_____
_____

Actions & Accomplishments I'm Grateful For Today (Big & Small):
_____
_____
_____
_____

Sources & Resources I'm Grateful For Today (Higher Power, Pets, Places, Things):
_____
_____
_____
_____

Friday _____
_{Date}

Experiences I'm Grateful For Today (Events, Opportunities, Moments, & Sensations):
_____
_____
_____

People I'm Grateful For Today (Interactions, Conversations, Kindnesses Given or Received):
_____
_____
_____

Actions & Accomplishments I'm Grateful For Today (Big & Small):
_____
_____
_____

Sources & Resources I'm Grateful For Today (Higher Power, Pets, Places, Things):
_____
_____
_____

Saturday _____
_{Date}

Experiences I'm Grateful For Today (Events, Opportunities, Moments, & Sensations):
_____
_____
_____

People I'm Grateful For Today (Interactions, Conversations, Kindnesses Given or Received):
_____
_____
_____

Actions & Accomplishments I'm Grateful For Today (Big & Small):
_____
_____
_____

Sources & Resources I'm Grateful For Today (Higher Power, Pets, Places, Things):
_____
_____
_____

Think Thankfully!
Week #34

"We are all more blind to what we have than to what we have not."
~ Audre Lorde

Highlights From The Research:

Froh, Emmons, Card, Bono, & Wilson studied high school students and found that adolescents who were grateful achieved higher GPAs, were more socially integrated, had greater life satisfaction, and were less envious and less depressed than adolescents with lower levels of gratitude.[34]

Who Will You Express Your Gratitude To This Week?

_____
_____

Sunday _____
                            Date

Experiences I'm Grateful For Today (Events, Opportunities, Moments, & Sensations):
_____
_____
_____
_____

People I'm Grateful For Today (Interactions, Conversations, Kindnesses Given or Received):
_____
_____
_____
_____

Actions & Accomplishments I'm Grateful For Today (Big & Small):
_____
_____
_____
_____

Sources & Resources I'm Grateful For Today (Higher Power, Pets, Places, Things):
_____
_____
_____
_____

Monday _____
Date

Experiences I'm Grateful For Today (Events, Opportunities, Moments, & Sensations):
_____
_____
_____
_____

People I'm Grateful For Today (Interactions, Conversations, Kindnesses Given or Received):
_____
_____
_____
_____

Actions & Accomplishments I'm Grateful For Today (Big & Small):
_____
_____
_____
_____

Sources & Resources I'm Grateful For Today (Higher Power, Pets, Places, Things):
_____
_____
_____
_____

Tuesday _____
Date

Experiences I'm Grateful For Today (Events, Opportunities, Moments, & Sensations):
_____
_____
_____
_____

People I'm Grateful For Today (Interactions, Conversations, Kindnesses Given or Received):
_____
_____
_____
_____

Actions & Accomplishments I'm Grateful For Today (Big & Small):
_____
_____
_____
_____

Sources & Resources I'm Grateful For Today (Higher Power, Pets, Places, Things):
_____
_____
_____
_____

Wednesday _____
Date

Experiences I'm Grateful For Today (Events, Opportunities, Moments, & Sensations):
_____
_____
_____
_____

People I'm Grateful For Today (Interactions, Conversations, Kindnesses Given or Received):
_____
_____
_____
_____

Actions & Accomplishments I'm Grateful For Today (Big & Small):
_____
_____
_____
_____

Sources & Resources I'm Grateful For Today (Higher Power, Pets, Places, Things):
_____
_____
_____
_____

Thursday _____
Date

Experiences I'm Grateful For Today (Events, Opportunities, Moments, & Sensations):
_____
_____
_____
_____

People I'm Grateful For Today (Interactions, Conversations, Kindnesses Given or Received):
_____
_____
_____
_____

Actions & Accomplishments I'm Grateful For Today (Big & Small):
_____
_____
_____
_____

Sources & Resources I'm Grateful For Today (Higher Power, Pets, Places, Things):
_____
_____
_____
_____

Friday _____
Date

Experiences I'm Grateful For Today (Events, Opportunities, Moments, & Sensations):
_____
_____
_____

People I'm Grateful For Today (Interactions, Conversations, Kindnesses Given or Received):
_____
_____
_____

Actions & Accomplishments I'm Grateful For Today (Big & Small):
_____
_____
_____

Sources & Resources I'm Grateful For Today (Higher Power, Pets, Places, Things):
_____
_____
_____

Saturday _____
Date

Experiences I'm Grateful For Today (Events, Opportunities, Moments, & Sensations):
_____
_____
_____

People I'm Grateful For Today (Interactions, Conversations, Kindnesses Given or Received):
_____
_____
_____

Actions & Accomplishments I'm Grateful For Today (Big & Small):
_____
_____
_____

Sources & Resources I'm Grateful For Today (Higher Power, Pets, Places, Things):
_____
_____
_____

Think Thankfully!
Week #35

"The deepest craving of human nature is the need to be appreciated."
~ William James

Highlights From The Research:

Wood, Joseph, & Linley conducted a study of adults and found that gratitude was related to seeking emotional and social support, positive reinterpretation of events and growth, active coping, and planning. They also found that those with higher levels of gratitude experienced less behavioral disengagement, self-blame, substance use, and denial. Furthermore, those with greater gratitude had higher levels of happiness and satisfaction with life, as well as lower levels of stress and depression.[35]

Who Will You Express Your Gratitude To This Week?

_____
_____

Sunday _____
                          Date

Experiences I'm Grateful For Today (Events, Opportunities, Moments, & Sensations):
_____
_____
_____
_____

People I'm Grateful For Today (Interactions, Conversations, Kindnesses Given or Received):
_____
_____
_____
_____

Actions & Accomplishments I'm Grateful For Today (Big & Small):
_____
_____
_____
_____

Sources & Resources I'm Grateful For Today (Higher Power, Pets, Places, Things):
_____
_____
_____
_____

Monday _____
                                    Date
Experiences I'm Grateful For Today (Events, Opportunities, Moments, & Sensations):
_____
_____
_____
_____

People I'm Grateful For Today (Interactions, Conversations, Kindnesses Given or Received):
_____
_____
_____
_____

Actions & Accomplishments I'm Grateful For Today (Big & Small):
_____
_____
_____
_____

Sources & Resources I'm Grateful For Today (Higher Power, Pets, Places, Things):
_____
_____
_____
_____

Tuesday _____
                                    Date
Experiences I'm Grateful For Today (Events, Opportunities, Moments, & Sensations):
_____
_____
_____
_____

People I'm Grateful For Today (Interactions, Conversations, Kindnesses Given or Received):
_____
_____
_____
_____

Actions & Accomplishments I'm Grateful For Today (Big & Small):
_____
_____
_____
_____

Sources & Resources I'm Grateful For Today (Higher Power, Pets, Places, Things):
_____
_____
_____
_____

Wednesday _____
_{Date}

Experiences I'm Grateful For Today (Events, Opportunities, Moments, & Sensations):
_____
_____
_____

People I'm Grateful For Today (Interactions, Conversations, Kindnesses Given or Received):
_____
_____
_____

Actions & Accomplishments I'm Grateful For Today (Big & Small):
_____
_____
_____

Sources & Resources I'm Grateful For Today (Higher Power, Pets, Places, Things):
_____
_____
_____

Thursday _____
_{Date}

Experiences I'm Grateful For Today (Events, Opportunities, Moments, & Sensations):
_____
_____
_____

People I'm Grateful For Today (Interactions, Conversations, Kindnesses Given or Received):
_____
_____
_____

Actions & Accomplishments I'm Grateful For Today (Big & Small):
_____
_____
_____

Sources & Resources I'm Grateful For Today (Higher Power, Pets, Places, Things):
_____
_____
_____

Friday _____
_{Date}

Experiences I'm Grateful For Today (Events, Opportunities, Moments, & Sensations):

_____
_____
_____

People I'm Grateful For Today (Interactions, Conversations, Kindnesses Given or Received):

_____
_____
_____

Actions & Accomplishments I'm Grateful For Today (Big & Small):

_____
_____
_____

Sources & Resources I'm Grateful For Today (Higher Power, Pets, Places, Things):

_____
_____
_____

Saturday _____
_{Date}

Experiences I'm Grateful For Today (Events, Opportunities, Moments, & Sensations):

_____
_____
_____

People I'm Grateful For Today (Interactions, Conversations, Kindnesses Given or Received):

_____
_____
_____

Actions & Accomplishments I'm Grateful For Today (Big & Small):

_____
_____
_____

Sources & Resources I'm Grateful For Today (Higher Power, Pets, Places, Things):

_____
_____
_____

Think Thankfully!
Week #36

"Do not spoil what you have by desiring what you have not; remember that what you now have was once among the things you only hoped for."
~ Epicurus

Highlights From The Research:

Vernon, Dillon, & Steiner examined the relationship between gratitude and posttraumatic stress disorder (PTSD) symptom severity for college women with trauma histories. They found that women who retrospectively reported higher levels of gratitude in response to trauma reported fewer and less severe PTSD symptoms months and years after the trauma.[36]

Who Will You Express Your Gratitude To This Week?
_____
_____

Sunday _____
     Date

Experiences I'm Grateful For Today (Events, Opportunities, Moments, & Sensations):
_____
_____
_____
_____

People I'm Grateful For Today (Interactions, Conversations, Kindnesses Given or Received):
_____
_____
_____
_____

Actions & Accomplishments I'm Grateful For Today (Big & Small):
_____
_____
_____
_____

Sources & Resources I'm Grateful For Today (Higher Power, Pets, Places, Things):
_____
_____
_____
_____

Monday _____
_{Date}

Experiences I'm Grateful For Today (Events, Opportunities, Moments, & Sensations):
_____
_____
_____

People I'm Grateful For Today (Interactions, Conversations, Kindnesses Given or Received):
_____
_____
_____

Actions & Accomplishments I'm Grateful For Today (Big & Small):
_____
_____
_____

Sources & Resources I'm Grateful For Today (Higher Power, Pets, Places, Things):
_____
_____
_____

Tuesday _____
_{Date}

Experiences I'm Grateful For Today (Events, Opportunities, Moments, & Sensations):
_____
_____
_____

People I'm Grateful For Today (Interactions, Conversations, Kindnesses Given or Received):
_____
_____
_____

Actions & Accomplishments I'm Grateful For Today (Big & Small):
_____
_____
_____

Sources & Resources I'm Grateful For Today (Higher Power, Pets, Places, Things):
_____
_____
_____

Wednesday _____

Date

Experiences I'm Grateful For Today (Events, Opportunities, Moments, & Sensations):
_____
_____
_____
_____

People I'm Grateful For Today (Interactions, Conversations, Kindnesses Given or Received):
_____
_____
_____
_____

Actions & Accomplishments I'm Grateful For Today (Big & Small):
_____
_____
_____
_____

Sources & Resources I'm Grateful For Today (Higher Power, Pets, Places, Things):
_____
_____
_____
_____

Thursday _____

Date

Experiences I'm Grateful For Today (Events, Opportunities, Moments, & Sensations):
_____
_____
_____
_____

People I'm Grateful For Today (Interactions, Conversations, Kindnesses Given or Received):
_____
_____
_____
_____

Actions & Accomplishments I'm Grateful For Today (Big & Small):
_____
_____
_____
_____

Sources & Resources I'm Grateful For Today (Higher Power, Pets, Places, Things):
_____
_____
_____
_____

Friday _____
Date

Experiences I'm Grateful For Today (Events, Opportunities, Moments, & Sensations):
_____
_____
_____

People I'm Grateful For Today (Interactions, Conversations, Kindnesses Given or Received):
_____
_____
_____

Actions & Accomplishments I'm Grateful For Today (Big & Small):
_____
_____
_____

Sources & Resources I'm Grateful For Today (Higher Power, Pets, Places, Things):
_____
_____
_____

Saturday _____
Date

Experiences I'm Grateful For Today (Events, Opportunities, Moments, & Sensations):
_____
_____
_____

People I'm Grateful For Today (Interactions, Conversations, Kindnesses Given or Received):
_____
_____
_____

Actions & Accomplishments I'm Grateful For Today (Big & Small):
_____
_____
_____

Sources & Resources I'm Grateful For Today (Higher Power, Pets, Places, Things):
_____
_____
_____

Think Thankfully!
Week #37

"When gratitude becomes an essential foundation in our lives, miracles start to appear everywhere."
~ Emmanuel Dagher

Highlights From The Research:

Ruini & Vescovelli conducted a study of breast cancer patients and found that those with higher levels of gratitude exhibited greater post-traumatic growth, positive relationships, positive emotions, relaxation, and contentment. Higher gratitude was also associated with lower levels of distress, anxiety, depression, hostility-irritability, and overall symptomatology.[37]

Who Will You Express Your Gratitude To This Week?
_____
_____

Sunday _____
                            Date

Experiences I'm Grateful For Today (Events, Opportunities, Moments, & Sensations):
_____
_____
_____
_____

People I'm Grateful For Today (Interactions, Conversations, Kindnesses Given or Received):
_____
_____
_____
_____

Actions & Accomplishments I'm Grateful For Today (Big & Small):
_____
_____
_____
_____

Sources & Resources I'm Grateful For Today (Higher Power, Pets, Places, Things):
_____
_____
_____
_____

Monday _____
_{Date}

Experiences I'm Grateful For Today (Events, Opportunities, Moments, & Sensations):
_____
_____
_____

People I'm Grateful For Today (Interactions, Conversations, Kindnesses Given or Received):
_____
_____
_____
_____

Actions & Accomplishments I'm Grateful For Today (Big & Small):
_____
_____
_____
_____

Sources & Resources I'm Grateful For Today (Higher Power, Pets, Places, Things):
_____
_____
_____

Tuesday _____
_{Date}

Experiences I'm Grateful For Today (Events, Opportunities, Moments, & Sensations):
_____
_____
_____

People I'm Grateful For Today (Interactions, Conversations, Kindnesses Given or Received):
_____
_____
_____
_____

Actions & Accomplishments I'm Grateful For Today (Big & Small):
_____
_____
_____
_____

Sources & Resources I'm Grateful For Today (Higher Power, Pets, Places, Things):
_____
_____
_____

Wednesday _____
_{Date}

Experiences I'm Grateful For Today (Events, Opportunities, Moments, & Sensations):

_____
_____
_____

People I'm Grateful For Today (Interactions, Conversations, Kindnesses Given or Received):

_____
_____
_____
_____

Actions & Accomplishments I'm Grateful For Today (Big & Small):

_____
_____
_____
_____

Sources & Resources I'm Grateful For Today (Higher Power, Pets, Places, Things):

_____
_____
_____
_____

Thursday _____
_{Date}

Experiences I'm Grateful For Today (Events, Opportunities, Moments, & Sensations):

_____
_____
_____

People I'm Grateful For Today (Interactions, Conversations, Kindnesses Given or Received):

_____
_____
_____
_____

Actions & Accomplishments I'm Grateful For Today (Big & Small):

_____
_____
_____
_____

Sources & Resources I'm Grateful For Today (Higher Power, Pets, Places, Things):

_____
_____
_____
_____

Friday _____
Date

Experiences I'm Grateful For Today (Events, Opportunities, Moments, & Sensations):
_____
_____
_____

People I'm Grateful For Today (Interactions, Conversations, Kindnesses Given or Received):
_____
_____
_____

Actions & Accomplishments I'm Grateful For Today (Big & Small):
_____
_____
_____

Sources & Resources I'm Grateful For Today (Higher Power, Pets, Places, Things):
_____
_____
_____

Saturday _____
Date

Experiences I'm Grateful For Today (Events, Opportunities, Moments, & Sensations):
_____
_____
_____

People I'm Grateful For Today (Interactions, Conversations, Kindnesses Given or Received):
_____
_____
_____

Actions & Accomplishments I'm Grateful For Today (Big & Small):
_____
_____
_____

Sources & Resources I'm Grateful For Today (Higher Power, Pets, Places, Things):
_____
_____
_____

Think Thankfully!
Week #38

"He is a wise man who does not grieve for the things which he has not but rejoices for those which he has."
~ Epictetus

Highlights From The Research:

Ng & Wong conducted a study of patients experiencing chronic pain and found that patients with chronic pain who reported higher levels of gratitude experienced less depression and anxiety, and better sleep.[38]

Who Will You Express Your Gratitude To This Week?

_____
_____

Sunday _____
_{Date}

Experiences I'm Grateful For Today (Events, Opportunities, Moments, & Sensations):
_____
_____
_____
_____

People I'm Grateful For Today (Interactions, Conversations, Kindnesses Given or Received):
_____
_____
_____
_____

Actions & Accomplishments I'm Grateful For Today (Big & Small):
_____
_____
_____
_____

Sources & Resources I'm Grateful For Today (Higher Power, Pets, Places, Things):
_____
_____
_____
_____

Monday _____
Date

Experiences I'm Grateful For Today (Events, Opportunities, Moments, & Sensations):
_____
_____
_____

People I'm Grateful For Today (Interactions, Conversations, Kindnesses Given or Received):
_____
_____
_____

Actions & Accomplishments I'm Grateful For Today (Big & Small):
_____
_____
_____

Sources & Resources I'm Grateful For Today (Higher Power, Pets, Places, Things):
_____
_____
_____

Tuesday _____
Date

Experiences I'm Grateful For Today (Events, Opportunities, Moments, & Sensations):
_____
_____
_____

People I'm Grateful For Today (Interactions, Conversations, Kindnesses Given or Received):
_____
_____
_____

Actions & Accomplishments I'm Grateful For Today (Big & Small):
_____
_____
_____

Sources & Resources I'm Grateful For Today (Higher Power, Pets, Places, Things):
_____
_____
_____

Wednesday _____
Date

Experiences I'm Grateful For Today (Events, Opportunities, Moments, & Sensations):
_____
_____
_____

People I'm Grateful For Today (Interactions, Conversations, Kindnesses Given or Received):
_____
_____
_____

Actions & Accomplishments I'm Grateful For Today (Big & Small):
_____
_____
_____

Sources & Resources I'm Grateful For Today (Higher Power, Pets, Places, Things):
_____
_____
_____

Thursday _____
Date

Experiences I'm Grateful For Today (Events, Opportunities, Moments, & Sensations):
_____
_____
_____

People I'm Grateful For Today (Interactions, Conversations, Kindnesses Given or Received):
_____
_____
_____

Actions & Accomplishments I'm Grateful For Today (Big & Small):
_____
_____
_____

Sources & Resources I'm Grateful For Today (Higher Power, Pets, Places, Things):
_____
_____
_____

Friday _____
Date

Experiences I'm Grateful For Today (Events, Opportunities, Moments, & Sensations):
_____
_____
_____
_____

People I'm Grateful For Today (Interactions, Conversations, Kindnesses Given or Received):
_____
_____
_____
_____

Actions & Accomplishments I'm Grateful For Today (Big & Small):
_____
_____
_____
_____

Sources & Resources I'm Grateful For Today (Higher Power, Pets, Places, Things):
_____
_____
_____
_____

Saturday _____
Date

Experiences I'm Grateful For Today (Events, Opportunities, Moments, & Sensations):
_____
_____
_____
_____

People I'm Grateful For Today (Interactions, Conversations, Kindnesses Given or Received):
_____
_____
_____
_____

Actions & Accomplishments I'm Grateful For Today (Big & Small):
_____
_____
_____
_____

Sources & Resources I'm Grateful For Today (Higher Power, Pets, Places, Things):
_____
_____
_____
_____

Think Thankfully!
Week #39

"Gratitude is a powerful process for shifting your energy and bringing more of what you want into your life. Be grateful for what you already have, and you will attract more good things."
~ Rhonda Byrne

Highlights From The Research:

Lai & O'Carroll conducted a study of adults who participated in a three-week gratitude intervention, listing three things they were grateful for daily. They found that practicing gratitude increases positive emotions.[39]

Who Will You Express Your Gratitude To This Week?
_____
_____

Sunday _____
                        Date

Experiences I'm Grateful For Today (Events, Opportunities, Moments, & Sensations):
_____
_____
_____
_____

People I'm Grateful For Today (Interactions, Conversations, Kindnesses Given or Received):
_____
_____
_____
_____

Actions & Accomplishments I'm Grateful For Today (Big & Small):
_____
_____
_____
_____

Sources & Resources I'm Grateful For Today (Higher Power, Pets, Places, Things):
_____
_____
_____
_____

Monday _____
_{Date}

Experiences I'm Grateful For Today (Events, Opportunities, Moments, & Sensations):
_____
_____
_____

People I'm Grateful For Today (Interactions, Conversations, Kindnesses Given or Received):
_____
_____
_____

Actions & Accomplishments I'm Grateful For Today (Big & Small):
_____
_____
_____

Sources & Resources I'm Grateful For Today (Higher Power, Pets, Places, Things):
_____
_____
_____

Tuesday _____
_{Date}

Experiences I'm Grateful For Today (Events, Opportunities, Moments, & Sensations):
_____
_____
_____

People I'm Grateful For Today (Interactions, Conversations, Kindnesses Given or Received):
_____
_____
_____

Actions & Accomplishments I'm Grateful For Today (Big & Small):
_____
_____
_____

Sources & Resources I'm Grateful For Today (Higher Power, Pets, Places, Things):
_____
_____
_____

Wednesday _____
_{Date}

Experiences I'm Grateful For Today (Events, Opportunities, Moments, & Sensations):
_____
_____
_____

People I'm Grateful For Today (Interactions, Conversations, Kindnesses Given or Received):
_____
_____
_____

Actions & Accomplishments I'm Grateful For Today (Big & Small):
_____
_____
_____

Sources & Resources I'm Grateful For Today (Higher Power, Pets, Places, Things):
_____
_____
_____

Thursday _____
_{Date}

Experiences I'm Grateful For Today (Events, Opportunities, Moments, & Sensations):
_____
_____
_____

People I'm Grateful For Today (Interactions, Conversations, Kindnesses Given or Received):
_____
_____
_____

Actions & Accomplishments I'm Grateful For Today (Big & Small):
_____
_____
_____

Sources & Resources I'm Grateful For Today (Higher Power, Pets, Places, Things):
_____
_____
_____

Friday _____
Date

Experiences I'm Grateful For Today (Events, Opportunities, Moments, & Sensations):
_____
_____
_____
_____

People I'm Grateful For Today (Interactions, Conversations, Kindnesses Given or Received):
_____
_____
_____
_____

Actions & Accomplishments I'm Grateful For Today (Big & Small):
_____
_____
_____
_____

Sources & Resources I'm Grateful For Today (Higher Power, Pets, Places, Things):
_____
_____
_____
_____

Saturday _____
Date

Experiences I'm Grateful For Today (Events, Opportunities, Moments, & Sensations):
_____
_____
_____
_____

People I'm Grateful For Today (Interactions, Conversations, Kindnesses Given or Received):
_____
_____
_____
_____

Actions & Accomplishments I'm Grateful For Today (Big & Small):
_____
_____
_____
_____

Sources & Resources I'm Grateful For Today (Higher Power, Pets, Places, Things):
_____
_____
_____
_____

Think Thankfully!
Week #40

"So much to savor, so much to be grateful for. And since I'm not sure of the address to which to send my gratitude, I put it out here in everything I do."
~ Michael J. Fox

Highlights From The Research:

Toepfer, Clehy, & Peters conducted a study of adults who wrote three letters of gratitude over a three-week period and found that this exercise boosted participants' happiness and life satisfaction, as well as decreased depressive symptoms.[40]

Who Will You Express Your Gratitude To This Week?
_____
_____

Sunday _____
                        Date

Experiences I'm Grateful For Today (Events, Opportunities, Moments, & Sensations):
_____
_____
_____
_____

People I'm Grateful For Today (Interactions, Conversations, Kindnesses Given or Received):
_____
_____
_____
_____

Actions & Accomplishments I'm Grateful For Today (Big & Small):
_____
_____
_____
_____

Sources & Resources I'm Grateful For Today (Higher Power, Pets, Places, Things):
_____
_____
_____
_____

Monday _____
_{Date}

Experiences I'm Grateful For Today (Events, Opportunities, Moments, & Sensations):
_____
_____
_____

People I'm Grateful For Today (Interactions, Conversations, Kindnesses Given or Received):
_____
_____
_____

Actions & Accomplishments I'm Grateful For Today (Big & Small):
_____
_____
_____

Sources & Resources I'm Grateful For Today (Higher Power, Pets, Places, Things):
_____
_____
_____

Tuesday _____
_{Date}

Experiences I'm Grateful For Today (Events, Opportunities, Moments, & Sensations):
_____
_____
_____

People I'm Grateful For Today (Interactions, Conversations, Kindnesses Given or Received):
_____
_____
_____

Actions & Accomplishments I'm Grateful For Today (Big & Small):
_____
_____
_____

Sources & Resources I'm Grateful For Today (Higher Power, Pets, Places, Things):
_____
_____
_____

Wednesday _____
Date

Experiences I'm Grateful For Today (Events, Opportunities, Moments, & Sensations):
_____
_____
_____
_____

People I'm Grateful For Today (Interactions, Conversations, Kindnesses Given or Received):
_____
_____
_____
_____

Actions & Accomplishments I'm Grateful For Today (Big & Small):
_____
_____
_____
_____

Sources & Resources I'm Grateful For Today (Higher Power, Pets, Places, Things):
_____
_____
_____
_____

Thursday _____
Date

Experiences I'm Grateful For Today (Events, Opportunities, Moments, & Sensations):
_____
_____
_____
_____

People I'm Grateful For Today (Interactions, Conversations, Kindnesses Given or Received):
_____
_____
_____
_____

Actions & Accomplishments I'm Grateful For Today (Big & Small):
_____
_____
_____
_____

Sources & Resources I'm Grateful For Today (Higher Power, Pets, Places, Things):
_____
_____
_____
_____

Friday _____
                          _{Date}

Experiences I'm Grateful For Today (Events, Opportunities, Moments, & Sensations):
_____
_____
_____

People I'm Grateful For Today (Interactions, Conversations, Kindnesses Given or Received):
_____
_____
_____

Actions & Accomplishments I'm Grateful For Today (Big & Small):
_____
_____
_____

Sources & Resources I'm Grateful For Today (Higher Power, Pets, Places, Things):
_____
_____
_____

Saturday _____
                           _{Date}

Experiences I'm Grateful For Today (Events, Opportunities, Moments, & Sensations):
_____
_____
_____

People I'm Grateful For Today (Interactions, Conversations, Kindnesses Given or Received):
_____
_____
_____

Actions & Accomplishments I'm Grateful For Today (Big & Small):
_____
_____
_____

Sources & Resources I'm Grateful For Today (Higher Power, Pets, Places, Things):
_____
_____
_____

Think Thankfully!
Week #41

*"Gratitude is one of the most medicinal emotions we can feel.
It elevates our moods and fills us with joy."
~ Sara Avant Stover*

Highlights From The Research:

Redwine, Henry, Pung, Wilson, Chinh, Knight, Jain, Rutledge, Greenberg, Maisel, & Mills conducted a study of cardiac patients who participated in an eight-week gratitude journaling intervention, listing three to five things they were grateful for daily. They found that gratitude journaling was associated with improved trait gratitude (recognizing gratitude-eliciting events and responding with grateful emotion) and reduced inflammation.[41]

Who Will You Express Your Gratitude To This Week?
_____
_____

Sunday _____
Date

Experiences I'm Grateful For Today (Events, Opportunities, Moments, & Sensations):
_____
_____
_____
_____

People I'm Grateful For Today (Interactions, Conversations, Kindnesses Given or Received):
_____
_____
_____
_____

Actions & Accomplishments I'm Grateful For Today (Big & Small):
_____
_____
_____
_____

Sources & Resources I'm Grateful For Today (Higher Power, Pets, Places, Things):
_____
_____
_____
_____

Monday _____
_{Date}

Experiences I'm Grateful For Today (Events, Opportunities, Moments, & Sensations):
_____
_____
_____

People I'm Grateful For Today (Interactions, Conversations, Kindnesses Given or Received):
_____
_____
_____

Actions & Accomplishments I'm Grateful For Today (Big & Small):
_____
_____
_____

Sources & Resources I'm Grateful For Today (Higher Power, Pets, Places, Things):
_____
_____
_____

Tuesday _____
_{Date}

Experiences I'm Grateful For Today (Events, Opportunities, Moments, & Sensations):
_____
_____
_____

People I'm Grateful For Today (Interactions, Conversations, Kindnesses Given or Received):
_____
_____
_____

Actions & Accomplishments I'm Grateful For Today (Big & Small):
_____
_____
_____

Sources & Resources I'm Grateful For Today (Higher Power, Pets, Places, Things):
_____
_____
_____

Wednesday _____
Date

Experiences I'm Grateful For Today (Events, Opportunities, Moments, & Sensations):
_____
_____
_____
_____

People I'm Grateful For Today (Interactions, Conversations, Kindnesses Given or Received):
_____
_____
_____
_____

Actions & Accomplishments I'm Grateful For Today (Big & Small):
_____
_____
_____
_____

Sources & Resources I'm Grateful For Today (Higher Power, Pets, Places, Things):
_____
_____
_____
_____

Thursday _____
Date

Experiences I'm Grateful For Today (Events, Opportunities, Moments, & Sensations):
_____
_____
_____
_____

People I'm Grateful For Today (Interactions, Conversations, Kindnesses Given or Received):
_____
_____
_____
_____

Actions & Accomplishments I'm Grateful For Today (Big & Small):
_____
_____
_____
_____

Sources & Resources I'm Grateful For Today (Higher Power, Pets, Places, Things):
_____
_____
_____
_____

Friday _____
Date

Experiences I'm Grateful For Today (Events, Opportunities, Moments, & Sensations):
_____
_____
_____

People I'm Grateful For Today (Interactions, Conversations, Kindnesses Given or Received):
_____
_____
_____

Actions & Accomplishments I'm Grateful For Today (Big & Small):
_____
_____
_____

Sources & Resources I'm Grateful For Today (Higher Power, Pets, Places, Things):
_____
_____
_____

Saturday _____
Date

Experiences I'm Grateful For Today (Events, Opportunities, Moments, & Sensations):
_____
_____
_____

People I'm Grateful For Today (Interactions, Conversations, Kindnesses Given or Received):
_____
_____
_____

Actions & Accomplishments I'm Grateful For Today (Big & Small):
_____
_____
_____

Sources & Resources I'm Grateful For Today (Higher Power, Pets, Places, Things):
_____
_____
_____

Think Thankfully!
Week #42

"Gratitude unlocks all that's blocking us from really feeling truthful, really feeling authentic and vulnerable and happy."
~ Gabrielle Bernstein

Highlights From The Research:

Schnitker & Richardson conducted a study of college students, having them list 10 things they were grateful for once a week for five weeks and pray their thanks aloud to God. They found that participants experienced a decrease in negative emotions, as well as increased positive emotions and feelings of hope.[42]

Who Will You Express Your Gratitude To This Week?
_____
_____

Sunday _____
                            Date

Experiences I'm Grateful For Today (Events, Opportunities, Moments, & Sensations):
_____
_____
_____
_____

People I'm Grateful For Today (Interactions, Conversations, Kindnesses Given or Received):
_____
_____
_____
_____

Actions & Accomplishments I'm Grateful For Today (Big & Small):
_____
_____
_____
_____

Sources & Resources I'm Grateful For Today (Higher Power, Pets, Places, Things):
_____
_____
_____
_____

Monday _____
Date

Experiences I'm Grateful For Today (Events, Opportunities, Moments, & Sensations):
_____
_____
_____

People I'm Grateful For Today (Interactions, Conversations, Kindnesses Given or Received):
_____
_____
_____

Actions & Accomplishments I'm Grateful For Today (Big & Small):
_____
_____
_____

Sources & Resources I'm Grateful For Today (Higher Power, Pets, Places, Things):
_____
_____
_____

Tuesday _____
Date

Experiences I'm Grateful For Today (Events, Opportunities, Moments, & Sensations):
_____
_____
_____

People I'm Grateful For Today (Interactions, Conversations, Kindnesses Given or Received):
_____
_____
_____

Actions & Accomplishments I'm Grateful For Today (Big & Small):
_____
_____
_____

Sources & Resources I'm Grateful For Today (Higher Power, Pets, Places, Things):
_____
_____
_____

Wednesday _____
                                         Date

Experiences I'm Grateful For Today (Events, Opportunities, Moments, & Sensations):
_____
_____
_____

People I'm Grateful For Today (Interactions, Conversations, Kindnesses Given or Received):
_____
_____
_____

Actions & Accomplishments I'm Grateful For Today (Big & Small):
_____
_____
_____

Sources & Resources I'm Grateful For Today (Higher Power, Pets, Places, Things):
_____
_____
_____

Thursday _____
                                         Date

Experiences I'm Grateful For Today (Events, Opportunities, Moments, & Sensations):
_____
_____
_____

People I'm Grateful For Today (Interactions, Conversations, Kindnesses Given or Received):
_____
_____
_____

Actions & Accomplishments I'm Grateful For Today (Big & Small):
_____
_____
_____

Sources & Resources I'm Grateful For Today (Higher Power, Pets, Places, Things):
_____
_____
_____

Friday _____
Date

Experiences I'm Grateful For Today (Events, Opportunities, Moments, & Sensations):
_____
_____
_____

People I'm Grateful For Today (Interactions, Conversations, Kindnesses Given or Received):
_____
_____
_____

Actions & Accomplishments I'm Grateful For Today (Big & Small):
_____
_____
_____

Sources & Resources I'm Grateful For Today (Higher Power, Pets, Places, Things):
_____
_____
_____

Saturday _____
Date

Experiences I'm Grateful For Today (Events, Opportunities, Moments, & Sensations):
_____
_____
_____

People I'm Grateful For Today (Interactions, Conversations, Kindnesses Given or Received):
_____
_____
_____

Actions & Accomplishments I'm Grateful For Today (Big & Small):
_____
_____
_____

Sources & Resources I'm Grateful For Today (Higher Power, Pets, Places, Things):
_____
_____
_____

Think Thankfully!
Week #43

"Gratitude is riches. Complaint is poverty."
~ Doris Day

Highlights From The Research:

Southwell & Gould conducted a study of individuals with anxiety disorders and depression, having participants list five things they were grateful for at least three times a week for three weeks. They found that keeping a gratitude journal led to decreases in depression, anxiety, stress, and sleep difficulties, as well as increases in overall well-being.[43]

Who Will You Express Your Gratitude To This Week?

_____
_____

Sunday _____
Date

Experiences I'm Grateful For Today (Events, Opportunities, Moments, & Sensations):
_____
_____
_____
_____

People I'm Grateful For Today (Interactions, Conversations, Kindnesses Given or Received):
_____
_____
_____
_____

Actions & Accomplishments I'm Grateful For Today (Big & Small):
_____
_____
_____
_____

Sources & Resources I'm Grateful For Today (Higher Power, Pets, Places, Things):
_____
_____
_____
_____

Monday _____
Date

Experiences I'm Grateful For Today (Events, Opportunities, Moments, & Sensations):
_____
_____
_____

People I'm Grateful For Today (Interactions, Conversations, Kindnesses Given or Received):
_____
_____
_____
_____

Actions & Accomplishments I'm Grateful For Today (Big & Small):
_____
_____
_____

Sources & Resources I'm Grateful For Today (Higher Power, Pets, Places, Things):
_____
_____
_____

Tuesday _____
Date

Experiences I'm Grateful For Today (Events, Opportunities, Moments, & Sensations):
_____
_____
_____

People I'm Grateful For Today (Interactions, Conversations, Kindnesses Given or Received):
_____
_____
_____
_____

Actions & Accomplishments I'm Grateful For Today (Big & Small):
_____
_____
_____

Sources & Resources I'm Grateful For Today (Higher Power, Pets, Places, Things):
_____
_____
_____

Wednesday _____
_{Date}

Experiences I'm Grateful For Today (Events, Opportunities, Moments, & Sensations):
_____
_____
_____

People I'm Grateful For Today (Interactions, Conversations, Kindnesses Given or Received):
_____
_____
_____
_____

Actions & Accomplishments I'm Grateful For Today (Big & Small):
_____
_____
_____
_____

Sources & Resources I'm Grateful For Today (Higher Power, Pets, Places, Things):
_____
_____
_____
_____

Thursday _____
_{Date}

Experiences I'm Grateful For Today (Events, Opportunities, Moments, & Sensations):
_____
_____
_____

People I'm Grateful For Today (Interactions, Conversations, Kindnesses Given or Received):
_____
_____
_____
_____

Actions & Accomplishments I'm Grateful For Today (Big & Small):
_____
_____
_____
_____

Sources & Resources I'm Grateful For Today (Higher Power, Pets, Places, Things):
_____
_____
_____
_____

Friday _____
Date

Experiences I'm Grateful For Today (Events, Opportunities, Moments, & Sensations):
_____
_____
_____

People I'm Grateful For Today (Interactions, Conversations, Kindnesses Given or Received):
_____
_____
_____

Actions & Accomplishments I'm Grateful For Today (Big & Small):
_____
_____
_____

Sources & Resources I'm Grateful For Today (Higher Power, Pets, Places, Things):
_____
_____
_____

Saturday _____
Date

Experiences I'm Grateful For Today (Events, Opportunities, Moments, & Sensations):
_____
_____
_____

People I'm Grateful For Today (Interactions, Conversations, Kindnesses Given or Received):
_____
_____
_____

Actions & Accomplishments I'm Grateful For Today (Big & Small):
_____
_____
_____

Sources & Resources I'm Grateful For Today (Higher Power, Pets, Places, Things):
_____
_____
_____

Think Thankfully!
Week #44

"As long as this exists, this sunshine and this cloudless sky, and as long as I can enjoy it, how can I be sad?"
~ Anne Frank

Highlights From The Research:

Wolfe & Patterson performed a study of college students experiencing dysfunctional eating and body dissatisfaction, where participants listed things they were grateful for daily for two weeks. They discovered that maintaining a gratitude journal led to increases in body esteem, as well as decreases in body dissatisfaction, dysfunctional eating, and depressive symptoms.[44]

Who Will You Express Your Gratitude To This Week?
_____
_____

Sunday _____
                        Date

Experiences I'm Grateful For Today (Events, Opportunities, Moments, & Sensations):
_____
_____
_____
_____

People I'm Grateful For Today (Interactions, Conversations, Kindnesses Given or Received):
_____
_____
_____
_____

Actions & Accomplishments I'm Grateful For Today (Big & Small):
_____
_____
_____
_____

Sources & Resources I'm Grateful For Today (Higher Power, Pets, Places, Things):
_____
_____
_____
_____

Monday _____
_{Date}

Experiences I'm Grateful For Today (Events, Opportunities, Moments, & Sensations):
_____
_____
_____

People I'm Grateful For Today (Interactions, Conversations, Kindnesses Given or Received):
_____
_____
_____
_____

Actions & Accomplishments I'm Grateful For Today (Big & Small):
_____
_____
_____
_____

Sources & Resources I'm Grateful For Today (Higher Power, Pets, Places, Things):
_____
_____
_____
_____

Tuesday _____
_{Date}

Experiences I'm Grateful For Today (Events, Opportunities, Moments, & Sensations):
_____
_____
_____

People I'm Grateful For Today (Interactions, Conversations, Kindnesses Given or Received):
_____
_____
_____
_____

Actions & Accomplishments I'm Grateful For Today (Big & Small):
_____
_____
_____
_____

Sources & Resources I'm Grateful For Today (Higher Power, Pets, Places, Things):
_____
_____
_____
_____

Wednesday _____
Date

Experiences I'm Grateful For Today (Events, Opportunities, Moments, & Sensations):
_____
_____
_____
_____

People I'm Grateful For Today (Interactions, Conversations, Kindnesses Given or Received):
_____
_____
_____
_____

Actions & Accomplishments I'm Grateful For Today (Big & Small):
_____
_____
_____
_____

Sources & Resources I'm Grateful For Today (Higher Power, Pets, Places, Things):
_____
_____
_____
_____

Thursday _____
Date

Experiences I'm Grateful For Today (Events, Opportunities, Moments, & Sensations):
_____
_____
_____
_____

People I'm Grateful For Today (Interactions, Conversations, Kindnesses Given or Received):
_____
_____
_____
_____

Actions & Accomplishments I'm Grateful For Today (Big & Small):
_____
_____
_____
_____

Sources & Resources I'm Grateful For Today (Higher Power, Pets, Places, Things):
_____
_____
_____
_____

Friday _____
Date

Experiences I'm Grateful For Today (Events, Opportunities, Moments, & Sensations):
_____
_____
_____

People I'm Grateful For Today (Interactions, Conversations, Kindnesses Given or Received):
_____
_____
_____

Actions & Accomplishments I'm Grateful For Today (Big & Small):
_____
_____
_____

Sources & Resources I'm Grateful For Today (Higher Power, Pets, Places, Things):
_____
_____
_____

Saturday _____
Date

Experiences I'm Grateful For Today (Events, Opportunities, Moments, & Sensations):
_____
_____
_____

People I'm Grateful For Today (Interactions, Conversations, Kindnesses Given or Received):
_____
_____
_____

Actions & Accomplishments I'm Grateful For Today (Big & Small):
_____
_____
_____

Sources & Resources I'm Grateful For Today (Higher Power, Pets, Places, Things):
_____
_____
_____

Think Thankfully!
Week #45

"Our favorite attitude should be gratitude."
~ Zig Ziglar

Highlights From The Research:

Wood, Joseph, Lloyd, & Atkins conducted a study of adults and found that an attitude of gratitude is correlated with better sleep quality and sleep duration, as well as reduced sleep latency (amount of time it takes to fall asleep) and daytime dysfunction.[45]

Who Will You Express Your Gratitude To This Week?

_____
_____

Sunday _____
Date

Experiences I'm Grateful For Today (Events, Opportunities, Moments, & Sensations):
_____
_____
_____
_____

People I'm Grateful For Today (Interactions, Conversations, Kindnesses Given or Received):
_____
_____
_____
_____

Actions & Accomplishments I'm Grateful For Today (Big & Small):
_____
_____
_____
_____

Sources & Resources I'm Grateful For Today (Higher Power, Pets, Places, Things):
_____
_____
_____
_____

Monday _____
_{Date}

Experiences I'm Grateful For Today (Events, Opportunities, Moments, & Sensations):
_____
_____
_____
_____

People I'm Grateful For Today (Interactions, Conversations, Kindnesses Given or Received):
_____
_____
_____
_____

Actions & Accomplishments I'm Grateful For Today (Big & Small):
_____
_____
_____
_____

Sources & Resources I'm Grateful For Today (Higher Power, Pets, Places, Things):
_____
_____
_____
_____

Tuesday _____
_{Date}

Experiences I'm Grateful For Today (Events, Opportunities, Moments, & Sensations):
_____
_____
_____
_____

People I'm Grateful For Today (Interactions, Conversations, Kindnesses Given or Received):
_____
_____
_____
_____

Actions & Accomplishments I'm Grateful For Today (Big & Small):
_____
_____
_____
_____

Sources & Resources I'm Grateful For Today (Higher Power, Pets, Places, Things):
_____
_____
_____
_____

Wednesday _____
Date

Experiences I'm Grateful For Today (Events, Opportunities, Moments, & Sensations):
_____
_____
_____

People I'm Grateful For Today (Interactions, Conversations, Kindnesses Given or Received):
_____
_____
_____
_____

Actions & Accomplishments I'm Grateful For Today (Big & Small):
_____
_____
_____
_____

Sources & Resources I'm Grateful For Today (Higher Power, Pets, Places, Things):
_____
_____
_____
_____

Thursday _____
Date

Experiences I'm Grateful For Today (Events, Opportunities, Moments, & Sensations):
_____
_____
_____

People I'm Grateful For Today (Interactions, Conversations, Kindnesses Given or Received):
_____
_____
_____
_____

Actions & Accomplishments I'm Grateful For Today (Big & Small):
_____
_____
_____
_____

Sources & Resources I'm Grateful For Today (Higher Power, Pets, Places, Things):
_____
_____
_____
_____

Friday _____
Date

Experiences I'm Grateful For Today (Events, Opportunities, Moments, & Sensations):
_____
_____
_____

People I'm Grateful For Today (Interactions, Conversations, Kindnesses Given or Received):
_____
_____
_____
_____

Actions & Accomplishments I'm Grateful For Today (Big & Small):
_____
_____
_____

Sources & Resources I'm Grateful For Today (Higher Power, Pets, Places, Things):
_____
_____
_____

Saturday _____
Date

Experiences I'm Grateful For Today (Events, Opportunities, Moments, & Sensations):
_____
_____
_____

People I'm Grateful For Today (Interactions, Conversations, Kindnesses Given or Received):
_____
_____
_____
_____

Actions & Accomplishments I'm Grateful For Today (Big & Small):
_____
_____
_____

Sources & Resources I'm Grateful For Today (Higher Power, Pets, Places, Things):
_____
_____
_____

Think Thankfully!
Week #46

"Gratitude is a divine emotion: it fills the heart, but not to bursting; it warms it, but not to fever."
~ Charlotte Brontë

Highlights From The Research:

Lambert, Clark, Durtschi, Fincham, & Graham conducted a three-week study of college students in which participants were asked to focus on going the extra mile to express gratitude to a friend verbally or in writing, telling them how much they appreciate something specific that their friend has done for them. They found that expressing gratitude enhanced participants' degree of motivation to respond to their friends' needs.[46]

Who Will You Express Your Gratitude To This Week?

Sunday _____
Date

Experiences I'm Grateful For Today (Events, Opportunities, Moments, & Sensations):

People I'm Grateful For Today (Interactions, Conversations, Kindnesses Given or Received):

Actions & Accomplishments I'm Grateful For Today (Big & Small):

Sources & Resources I'm Grateful For Today (Higher Power, Pets, Places, Things):

Monday _____
                                    Date

Experiences I'm Grateful For Today (Events, Opportunities, Moments, & Sensations):
_____
_____
_____

People I'm Grateful For Today (Interactions, Conversations, Kindnesses Given or Received):
_____
_____
_____

Actions & Accomplishments I'm Grateful For Today (Big & Small):
_____
_____
_____

Sources & Resources I'm Grateful For Today (Higher Power, Pets, Places, Things):
_____
_____
_____

Tuesday _____
                                    Date

Experiences I'm Grateful For Today (Events, Opportunities, Moments, & Sensations):
_____
_____
_____

People I'm Grateful For Today (Interactions, Conversations, Kindnesses Given or Received):
_____
_____
_____

Actions & Accomplishments I'm Grateful For Today (Big & Small):
_____
_____
_____

Sources & Resources I'm Grateful For Today (Higher Power, Pets, Places, Things):
_____
_____
_____

Wednesday _____
Date

Experiences I'm Grateful For Today (Events, Opportunities, Moments, & Sensations):
_____
_____
_____
_____

People I'm Grateful For Today (Interactions, Conversations, Kindnesses Given or Received):
_____
_____
_____
_____

Actions & Accomplishments I'm Grateful For Today (Big & Small):
_____
_____
_____
_____

Sources & Resources I'm Grateful For Today (Higher Power, Pets, Places, Things):
_____
_____
_____
_____

Thursday _____
Date

Experiences I'm Grateful For Today (Events, Opportunities, Moments, & Sensations):
_____
_____
_____
_____

People I'm Grateful For Today (Interactions, Conversations, Kindnesses Given or Received):
_____
_____
_____
_____

Actions & Accomplishments I'm Grateful For Today (Big & Small):
_____
_____
_____
_____

Sources & Resources I'm Grateful For Today (Higher Power, Pets, Places, Things):
_____
_____
_____
_____

Friday _____
Date

Experiences I'm Grateful For Today (Events, Opportunities, Moments, & Sensations):
_____
_____
_____

People I'm Grateful For Today (Interactions, Conversations, Kindnesses Given or Received):
_____
_____
_____
_____

Actions & Accomplishments I'm Grateful For Today (Big & Small):
_____
_____
_____
_____

Sources & Resources I'm Grateful For Today (Higher Power, Pets, Places, Things):
_____
_____
_____
_____

Saturday _____
Date

Experiences I'm Grateful For Today (Events, Opportunities, Moments, & Sensations):
_____
_____
_____

People I'm Grateful For Today (Interactions, Conversations, Kindnesses Given or Received):
_____
_____
_____
_____

Actions & Accomplishments I'm Grateful For Today (Big & Small):
_____
_____
_____
_____

Sources & Resources I'm Grateful For Today (Higher Power, Pets, Places, Things):
_____
_____
_____
_____

Think Thankfully!
Week #47

*"The soul that gives thanks can find comfort in everything;
the soul that complains can find comfort in nothing."*
~ Hannah Whitall Smith

Highlights From The Research:

Kini, Wong, McInnis, Gabana, & Brown studied adults starting counseling for depression and/or anxiety, having participants write letters expressing gratitude. After three months, participants performed a "Pay It Forward" task in an fMRI scanner where they were given a monetary gift and asked to pass it on to a charitable cause to the extent that they felt grateful for the gift. They found that participants who wrote gratitude letters showed behavioral increases in gratitude and significantly greater neural modulation by gratitude in the medial prefrontal cortex.[47]

Who Will You Express Your Gratitude To This Week?

_____
_____

Sunday _____

Date

Experiences I'm Grateful For Today (Events, Opportunities, Moments, & Sensations):
_____
_____
_____
_____

People I'm Grateful For Today (Interactions, Conversations, Kindnesses Given or Received):
_____
_____
_____
_____

Actions & Accomplishments I'm Grateful For Today (Big & Small):
_____
_____
_____
_____

Sources & Resources I'm Grateful For Today (Higher Power, Pets, Places, Things):
_____
_____
_____
_____

Monday _____
_{Date}

Experiences I'm Grateful For Today (Events, Opportunities, Moments, & Sensations):
_____
_____
_____

People I'm Grateful For Today (Interactions, Conversations, Kindnesses Given or Received):
_____
_____
_____

Actions & Accomplishments I'm Grateful For Today (Big & Small):
_____
_____
_____

Sources & Resources I'm Grateful For Today (Higher Power, Pets, Places, Things):
_____
_____
_____

Tuesday _____
_{Date}

Experiences I'm Grateful For Today (Events, Opportunities, Moments, & Sensations):
_____
_____
_____

People I'm Grateful For Today (Interactions, Conversations, Kindnesses Given or Received):
_____
_____
_____

Actions & Accomplishments I'm Grateful For Today (Big & Small):
_____
_____
_____

Sources & Resources I'm Grateful For Today (Higher Power, Pets, Places, Things):
_____
_____
_____

Wednesday _____
Date

Experiences I'm Grateful For Today (Events, Opportunities, Moments, & Sensations):
_____
_____
_____
_____

People I'm Grateful For Today (Interactions, Conversations, Kindnesses Given or Received):
_____
_____
_____
_____

Actions & Accomplishments I'm Grateful For Today (Big & Small):
_____
_____
_____
_____

Sources & Resources I'm Grateful For Today (Higher Power, Pets, Places, Things):
_____
_____
_____
_____

Thursday _____
Date

Experiences I'm Grateful For Today (Events, Opportunities, Moments, & Sensations):
_____
_____
_____
_____

People I'm Grateful For Today (Interactions, Conversations, Kindnesses Given or Received):
_____
_____
_____
_____

Actions & Accomplishments I'm Grateful For Today (Big & Small):
_____
_____
_____
_____

Sources & Resources I'm Grateful For Today (Higher Power, Pets, Places, Things):
_____
_____
_____
_____

Friday _____
_____Date
Experiences I'm Grateful For Today (Events, Opportunities, Moments, & Sensations):
_____
_____
_____

People I'm Grateful For Today (Interactions, Conversations, Kindnesses Given or Received):
_____
_____
_____

Actions & Accomplishments I'm Grateful For Today (Big & Small):
_____
_____
_____

Sources & Resources I'm Grateful For Today (Higher Power, Pets, Places, Things):
_____
_____
_____

Saturday _____
_____Date
Experiences I'm Grateful For Today (Events, Opportunities, Moments, & Sensations):
_____
_____
_____

People I'm Grateful For Today (Interactions, Conversations, Kindnesses Given or Received):
_____
_____
_____

Actions & Accomplishments I'm Grateful For Today (Big & Small):
_____
_____
_____

Sources & Resources I'm Grateful For Today (Higher Power, Pets, Places, Things):
_____
_____
_____

Think Thankfully!
Week #48

*"Gratitude is a powerful catalyst for happiness.
It's the spark that lights a fire of joy in your soul."*
~ Amy Collette

Highlights From The Research:

Rash, Matsuba, & Prkachin conducted a study of adults in which participants were asked to contemplate items, people, or events that they were grateful for, concentrate on the feelings of gratitude associated with the contemplation, and write down their grateful experiences in a journal. They performed this reflection process twice a week for four weeks. The study found that contemplating gratitude was correlated with greater satisfaction with life and higher self-esteem.[48]

Who Will You Express Your Gratitude To This Week?
_____
_____

Sunday _____
                                                        Date

Experiences I'm Grateful For Today (Events, Opportunities, Moments, & Sensations):
_____
_____
_____
_____

People I'm Grateful For Today (Interactions, Conversations, Kindnesses Given or Received):
_____
_____
_____
_____

Actions & Accomplishments I'm Grateful For Today (Big & Small):
_____
_____
_____
_____

Sources & Resources I'm Grateful For Today (Higher Power, Pets, Places, Things):
_____
_____
_____
_____

Monday _____
Date

Experiences I'm Grateful For Today (Events, Opportunities, Moments, & Sensations):
_____
_____
_____

People I'm Grateful For Today (Interactions, Conversations, Kindnesses Given or Received):
_____
_____
_____

Actions & Accomplishments I'm Grateful For Today (Big & Small):
_____
_____
_____

Sources & Resources I'm Grateful For Today (Higher Power, Pets, Places, Things):
_____
_____
_____

Tuesday _____
Date

Experiences I'm Grateful For Today (Events, Opportunities, Moments, & Sensations):
_____
_____
_____

People I'm Grateful For Today (Interactions, Conversations, Kindnesses Given or Received):
_____
_____
_____

Actions & Accomplishments I'm Grateful For Today (Big & Small):
_____
_____
_____

Sources & Resources I'm Grateful For Today (Higher Power, Pets, Places, Things):
_____
_____
_____

Wednesday _____
Date

Experiences I'm Grateful For Today (Events, Opportunities, Moments, & Sensations):
_____
_____
_____
_____

People I'm Grateful For Today (Interactions, Conversations, Kindnesses Given or Received):
_____
_____
_____
_____

Actions & Accomplishments I'm Grateful For Today (Big & Small):
_____
_____
_____
_____

Sources & Resources I'm Grateful For Today (Higher Power, Pets, Places, Things):
_____
_____
_____
_____

Thursday _____
Date

Experiences I'm Grateful For Today (Events, Opportunities, Moments, & Sensations):
_____
_____
_____
_____

People I'm Grateful For Today (Interactions, Conversations, Kindnesses Given or Received):
_____
_____
_____
_____

Actions & Accomplishments I'm Grateful For Today (Big & Small):
_____
_____
_____
_____

Sources & Resources I'm Grateful For Today (Higher Power, Pets, Places, Things):
_____
_____
_____
_____

Friday _____
_{Date}

Experiences I'm Grateful For Today (Events, Opportunities, Moments, & Sensations):
_____
_____
_____
_____

People I'm Grateful For Today (Interactions, Conversations, Kindnesses Given or Received):
_____
_____
_____
_____

Actions & Accomplishments I'm Grateful For Today (Big & Small):
_____
_____
_____
_____

Sources & Resources I'm Grateful For Today (Higher Power, Pets, Places, Things):
_____
_____
_____
_____

Saturday _____
_{Date}

Experiences I'm Grateful For Today (Events, Opportunities, Moments, & Sensations):
_____
_____
_____
_____

People I'm Grateful For Today (Interactions, Conversations, Kindnesses Given or Received):
_____
_____
_____
_____

Actions & Accomplishments I'm Grateful For Today (Big & Small):
_____
_____
_____
_____

Sources & Resources I'm Grateful For Today (Higher Power, Pets, Places, Things):
_____
_____
_____
_____

Think Thankfully!
Week #49

*"I lie in bed at night, after ending my prayers with the words
'Ich danke dir für all das Gute und Liebe und Schöne.'
(Thank you, Higher Power, for all that is good and dear and beautiful.)"*
~ Anne Frank

Highlights From The Research:

Kardaş, Çam, Eşkisu, & Gelibolu conducted a study of college students and discovered that of all traits studied – gratitude, hope, optimism, and life satisfaction – an attitude of gratitude was the greatest predictor of psychological well-being.[49]

Who Will You Express Your Gratitude To This Week?

_____
_____

Sunday _____
                                Date

Experiences I'm Grateful For Today (Events, Opportunities, Moments, & Sensations):
_____
_____
_____
_____

People I'm Grateful For Today (Interactions, Conversations, Kindnesses Given or Received):
_____
_____
_____
_____

Actions & Accomplishments I'm Grateful For Today (Big & Small):
_____
_____
_____
_____

Sources & Resources I'm Grateful For Today (Higher Power, Pets, Places, Things):
_____
_____
_____
_____

Monday _____
_{Date}

Experiences I'm Grateful For Today (Events, Opportunities, Moments, & Sensations):
_____
_____
_____
_____

People I'm Grateful For Today (Interactions, Conversations, Kindnesses Given or Received):
_____
_____
_____
_____

Actions & Accomplishments I'm Grateful For Today (Big & Small):
_____
_____
_____
_____

Sources & Resources I'm Grateful For Today (Higher Power, Pets, Places, Things):
_____
_____
_____
_____

Tuesday _____
_{Date}

Experiences I'm Grateful For Today (Events, Opportunities, Moments, & Sensations):
_____
_____
_____
_____

People I'm Grateful For Today (Interactions, Conversations, Kindnesses Given or Received):
_____
_____
_____
_____

Actions & Accomplishments I'm Grateful For Today (Big & Small):
_____
_____
_____
_____

Sources & Resources I'm Grateful For Today (Higher Power, Pets, Places, Things):
_____
_____
_____
_____

Wednesday _____
Date

Experiences I'm Grateful For Today (Events, Opportunities, Moments, & Sensations):
_____
_____
_____

People I'm Grateful For Today (Interactions, Conversations, Kindnesses Given or Received):
_____
_____
_____
_____

Actions & Accomplishments I'm Grateful For Today (Big & Small):
_____
_____
_____
_____

Sources & Resources I'm Grateful For Today (Higher Power, Pets, Places, Things):
_____
_____
_____
_____

Thursday _____
Date

Experiences I'm Grateful For Today (Events, Opportunities, Moments, & Sensations):
_____
_____
_____

People I'm Grateful For Today (Interactions, Conversations, Kindnesses Given or Received):
_____
_____
_____
_____

Actions & Accomplishments I'm Grateful For Today (Big & Small):
_____
_____
_____
_____

Sources & Resources I'm Grateful For Today (Higher Power, Pets, Places, Things):
_____
_____
_____
_____

Friday _____
Date

Experiences I'm Grateful For Today (Events, Opportunities, Moments, & Sensations):
_____
_____
_____

People I'm Grateful For Today (Interactions, Conversations, Kindnesses Given or Received):
_____
_____
_____

Actions & Accomplishments I'm Grateful For Today (Big & Small):
_____
_____
_____

Sources & Resources I'm Grateful For Today (Higher Power, Pets, Places, Things):
_____
_____
_____

Saturday _____
Date

Experiences I'm Grateful For Today (Events, Opportunities, Moments, & Sensations):
_____
_____
_____

People I'm Grateful For Today (Interactions, Conversations, Kindnesses Given or Received):
_____
_____
_____

Actions & Accomplishments I'm Grateful For Today (Big & Small):
_____
_____
_____

Sources & Resources I'm Grateful For Today (Higher Power, Pets, Places, Things):
_____
_____
_____

Think Thankfully!
Week #50

"You simply will not be the same person two months from now after consciously giving thanks each day for the abundance that exists in your life. And you will have set in motion an ancient spiritual law: the more you have and are grateful for, the more will be given you."
~ Sarah Ban Breathnach

Highlights From The Research:

Salvador-Ferrer conducted a study of college students and found that gratitude significantly predicts life satisfaction on both psychological and physical well-being.[50]

Who Will You Express Your Gratitude To This Week?

_____
_____

Sunday _____

Date

Experiences I'm Grateful For Today (Events, Opportunities, Moments, & Sensations):
_____
_____
_____
_____

People I'm Grateful For Today (Interactions, Conversations, Kindnesses Given or Received):
_____
_____
_____
_____

Actions & Accomplishments I'm Grateful For Today (Big & Small):
_____
_____
_____
_____

Sources & Resources I'm Grateful For Today (Higher Power, Pets, Places, Things):
_____
_____
_____
_____

Monday _____
Date

Experiences I'm Grateful For Today (Events, Opportunities, Moments, & Sensations):
_____
_____
_____
_____

People I'm Grateful For Today (Interactions, Conversations, Kindnesses Given or Received):
_____
_____
_____
_____

Actions & Accomplishments I'm Grateful For Today (Big & Small):
_____
_____
_____
_____

Sources & Resources I'm Grateful For Today (Higher Power, Pets, Places, Things):
_____
_____
_____
_____

Tuesday _____
Date

Experiences I'm Grateful For Today (Events, Opportunities, Moments, & Sensations):
_____
_____
_____
_____

People I'm Grateful For Today (Interactions, Conversations, Kindnesses Given or Received):
_____
_____
_____
_____

Actions & Accomplishments I'm Grateful For Today (Big & Small):
_____
_____
_____
_____

Sources & Resources I'm Grateful For Today (Higher Power, Pets, Places, Things):
_____
_____
_____
_____

Wednesday _____
Date

Experiences I'm Grateful For Today (Events, Opportunities, Moments, & Sensations):
_____
_____
_____
_____

People I'm Grateful For Today (Interactions, Conversations, Kindnesses Given or Received):
_____
_____
_____
_____

Actions & Accomplishments I'm Grateful For Today (Big & Small):
_____
_____
_____
_____

Sources & Resources I'm Grateful For Today (Higher Power, Pets, Places, Things):
_____
_____
_____
_____

Thursday _____
Date

Experiences I'm Grateful For Today (Events, Opportunities, Moments, & Sensations):
_____
_____
_____
_____

People I'm Grateful For Today (Interactions, Conversations, Kindnesses Given or Received):
_____
_____
_____
_____

Actions & Accomplishments I'm Grateful For Today (Big & Small):
_____
_____
_____
_____

Sources & Resources I'm Grateful For Today (Higher Power, Pets, Places, Things):
_____
_____
_____
_____

Friday _____
Date

Experiences I'm Grateful For Today (Events, Opportunities, Moments, & Sensations):
_____
_____
_____

People I'm Grateful For Today (Interactions, Conversations, Kindnesses Given or Received):
_____
_____
_____

Actions & Accomplishments I'm Grateful For Today (Big & Small):
_____
_____
_____

Sources & Resources I'm Grateful For Today (Higher Power, Pets, Places, Things):
_____
_____
_____

Saturday _____
Date

Experiences I'm Grateful For Today (Events, Opportunities, Moments, & Sensations):
_____
_____
_____

People I'm Grateful For Today (Interactions, Conversations, Kindnesses Given or Received):
_____
_____
_____

Actions & Accomplishments I'm Grateful For Today (Big & Small):
_____
_____
_____

Sources & Resources I'm Grateful For Today (Higher Power, Pets, Places, Things):
_____
_____
_____

Think Thankfully!
Week #51

"Acknowledging the good that you already have in your life is the foundation for all abundance."
~ Eckhart Tolle

Highlights From The Research:

vanOyen Witvliet, Richie, Root Luna, & Van Tongeren conducted a study of college students and found that gratitude exceeded all other characteristics studied, including forgivingness, patience, and self-control, in predicting participants' feelings of hope and happiness.[51]

Who Will You Express Your Gratitude To This Week?

___

Sunday _____
                                    Date

Experiences I'm Grateful For Today (Events, Opportunities, Moments, & Sensations):

___

People I'm Grateful For Today (Interactions, Conversations, Kindnesses Given or Received):

___

Actions & Accomplishments I'm Grateful For Today (Big & Small):

___

Sources & Resources I'm Grateful For Today (Higher Power, Pets, Places, Things):

Monday _____
Date

Experiences I'm Grateful For Today (Events, Opportunities, Moments, & Sensations):
_____
_____
_____
_____

People I'm Grateful For Today (Interactions, Conversations, Kindnesses Given or Received):
_____
_____
_____
_____

Actions & Accomplishments I'm Grateful For Today (Big & Small):
_____
_____
_____
_____

Sources & Resources I'm Grateful For Today (Higher Power, Pets, Places, Things):
_____
_____
_____
_____

Tuesday _____
Date

Experiences I'm Grateful For Today (Events, Opportunities, Moments, & Sensations):
_____
_____
_____
_____

People I'm Grateful For Today (Interactions, Conversations, Kindnesses Given or Received):
_____
_____
_____
_____

Actions & Accomplishments I'm Grateful For Today (Big & Small):
_____
_____
_____
_____

Sources & Resources I'm Grateful For Today (Higher Power, Pets, Places, Things):
_____
_____
_____
_____

Wednesday _____
_{Date}

Experiences I'm Grateful For Today (Events, Opportunities, Moments, & Sensations):
_____
_____
_____
_____

People I'm Grateful For Today (Interactions, Conversations, Kindnesses Given or Received):
_____
_____
_____
_____

Actions & Accomplishments I'm Grateful For Today (Big & Small):
_____
_____
_____
_____

Sources & Resources I'm Grateful For Today (Higher Power, Pets, Places, Things):
_____
_____
_____
_____

Thursday _____
_{Date}

Experiences I'm Grateful For Today (Events, Opportunities, Moments, & Sensations):
_____
_____
_____
_____

People I'm Grateful For Today (Interactions, Conversations, Kindnesses Given or Received):
_____
_____
_____
_____

Actions & Accomplishments I'm Grateful For Today (Big & Small):
_____
_____
_____
_____

Sources & Resources I'm Grateful For Today (Higher Power, Pets, Places, Things):
_____
_____
_____
_____

Friday _____
_{Date}

Experiences I'm Grateful For Today (Events, Opportunities, Moments, & Sensations):
_____
_____
_____

People I'm Grateful For Today (Interactions, Conversations, Kindnesses Given or Received):
_____
_____
_____

Actions & Accomplishments I'm Grateful For Today (Big & Small):
_____
_____
_____

Sources & Resources I'm Grateful For Today (Higher Power, Pets, Places, Things):
_____
_____
_____

Saturday _____
_{Date}

Experiences I'm Grateful For Today (Events, Opportunities, Moments, & Sensations):
_____
_____
_____

People I'm Grateful For Today (Interactions, Conversations, Kindnesses Given or Received):
_____
_____
_____

Actions & Accomplishments I'm Grateful For Today (Big & Small):
_____
_____
_____

Sources & Resources I'm Grateful For Today (Higher Power, Pets, Places, Things):
_____
_____
_____

Think Thankfully!
Week #52

"I started out giving thanks for small things, and the more thankful I became, the more my bounty increased. That's because — for sure — what you focus on expands. When you focus on the goodness in life, you create more of it."
~ Oprah Winfrey

Highlights From The Research:

Wilson conducted a study of college students in which students were reminded and encouraged via text messages sent every four to five days for three months, to engage in gratitude practices related to their learning. The study discovered that practicing gratitude toward learning supports students' ability to focus while in class and remain resilient when facing learning challenges.[52]

Who Will You Express Your Gratitude To This Week?

_____
_____

Sunday _____

Date

Experiences I'm Grateful For Today (Events, Opportunities, Moments, & Sensations):
_____
_____
_____
_____

People I'm Grateful For Today (Interactions, Conversations, Kindnesses Given or Received):
_____
_____
_____
_____

Actions & Accomplishments I'm Grateful For Today (Big & Small):
_____
_____
_____
_____

Sources & Resources I'm Grateful For Today (Higher Power, Pets, Places, Things):
_____
_____
_____
_____

Monday _____
Date

Experiences I'm Grateful For Today (Events, Opportunities, Moments, & Sensations):
_____
_____
_____

People I'm Grateful For Today (Interactions, Conversations, Kindnesses Given or Received):
_____
_____
_____

Actions & Accomplishments I'm Grateful For Today (Big & Small):
_____
_____
_____

Sources & Resources I'm Grateful For Today (Higher Power, Pets, Places, Things):
_____
_____
_____

Tuesday _____
Date

Experiences I'm Grateful For Today (Events, Opportunities, Moments, & Sensations):
_____
_____
_____

People I'm Grateful For Today (Interactions, Conversations, Kindnesses Given or Received):
_____
_____
_____

Actions & Accomplishments I'm Grateful For Today (Big & Small):
_____
_____
_____

Sources & Resources I'm Grateful For Today (Higher Power, Pets, Places, Things):
_____
_____
_____

Wednesday _____
Date

Experiences I'm Grateful For Today (Events, Opportunities, Moments, & Sensations):
_____
_____
_____
_____

People I'm Grateful For Today (Interactions, Conversations, Kindnesses Given or Received):
_____
_____
_____
_____

Actions & Accomplishments I'm Grateful For Today (Big & Small):
_____
_____
_____
_____

Sources & Resources I'm Grateful For Today (Higher Power, Pets, Places, Things):
_____
_____
_____
_____

Thursday _____
Date

Experiences I'm Grateful For Today (Events, Opportunities, Moments, & Sensations):
_____
_____
_____
_____

People I'm Grateful For Today (Interactions, Conversations, Kindnesses Given or Received):
_____
_____
_____
_____

Actions & Accomplishments I'm Grateful For Today (Big & Small):
_____
_____
_____
_____

Sources & Resources I'm Grateful For Today (Higher Power, Pets, Places, Things):
_____
_____
_____
_____

Friday _____
_{Date}

Experiences I'm Grateful For Today (Events, Opportunities, Moments, & Sensations):
_____
_____
_____
_____

People I'm Grateful For Today (Interactions, Conversations, Kindnesses Given or Received):
_____
_____
_____
_____

Actions & Accomplishments I'm Grateful For Today (Big & Small):
_____
_____
_____
_____

Sources & Resources I'm Grateful For Today (Higher Power, Pets, Places, Things):
_____
_____
_____
_____

Saturday _____
_{Date}

Experiences I'm Grateful For Today (Events, Opportunities, Moments, & Sensations):
_____
_____
_____
_____

People I'm Grateful For Today (Interactions, Conversations, Kindnesses Given or Received):
_____
_____
_____
_____

Actions & Accomplishments I'm Grateful For Today (Big & Small):
_____
_____
_____
_____

Sources & Resources I'm Grateful For Today (Higher Power, Pets, Places, Things):
_____
_____
_____
_____

Think Thankfully!
Bonus Week

"Gratitude for the present moment and the fullness of life now is the true prosperity."
~ Eckhart Tolle

Highlights From The Research:

Kloos, Austin, van't Klooster, Drossaert, & Bohlmeijer conducted a study of adults and found those who utilized a gratitude app for six weeks that incorporated writing about the good things in their lives, expressing gratitude toward others, and finding the positive during adversity were less depressed, anxious, and stressed and experienced less rumination, more positive reframing, and more gratitude.[53]

Who Will You Express Your Gratitude To This Week?
_____
_____

Sunday _____
_{Date}

Experiences I'm Grateful For Today (Events, Opportunities, Moments, & Sensations):
_____
_____
_____
_____

People I'm Grateful For Today (Interactions, Conversations, Kindnesses Given or Received):
_____
_____
_____
_____

Actions & Accomplishments I'm Grateful For Today (Big & Small):
_____
_____
_____
_____

Sources & Resources I'm Grateful For Today (Higher Power, Pets, Places, Things):
_____
_____
_____
_____

Monday _____
_{Date}

Experiences I'm Grateful For Today (Events, Opportunities, Moments, & Sensations):
_____
_____
_____
_____

People I'm Grateful For Today (Interactions, Conversations, Kindnesses Given or Received):
_____
_____
_____
_____

Actions & Accomplishments I'm Grateful For Today (Big & Small):
_____
_____
_____
_____

Sources & Resources I'm Grateful For Today (Higher Power, Pets, Places, Things):
_____
_____
_____
_____

Tuesday _____
_{Date}

Experiences I'm Grateful For Today (Events, Opportunities, Moments, & Sensations):
_____
_____
_____
_____

People I'm Grateful For Today (Interactions, Conversations, Kindnesses Given or Received):
_____
_____
_____
_____

Actions & Accomplishments I'm Grateful For Today (Big & Small):
_____
_____
_____
_____

Sources & Resources I'm Grateful For Today (Higher Power, Pets, Places, Things):
_____
_____
_____
_____

Wednesday _____
Date

Experiences I'm Grateful For Today (Events, Opportunities, Moments, & Sensations):
_____
_____
_____

People I'm Grateful For Today (Interactions, Conversations, Kindnesses Given or Received):
_____
_____
_____

Actions & Accomplishments I'm Grateful For Today (Big & Small):
_____
_____
_____

Sources & Resources I'm Grateful For Today (Higher Power, Pets, Places, Things):
_____
_____
_____

Thursday _____
Date

Experiences I'm Grateful For Today (Events, Opportunities, Moments, & Sensations):
_____
_____
_____

People I'm Grateful For Today (Interactions, Conversations, Kindnesses Given or Received):
_____
_____
_____

Actions & Accomplishments I'm Grateful For Today (Big & Small):
_____
_____
_____

Sources & Resources I'm Grateful For Today (Higher Power, Pets, Places, Things):
_____
_____
_____

Friday _____
Date

Experiences I'm Grateful For Today (Events, Opportunities, Moments, & Sensations):
_____
_____
_____

People I'm Grateful For Today (Interactions, Conversations, Kindnesses Given or Received):
_____
_____
_____

Actions & Accomplishments I'm Grateful For Today (Big & Small):
_____
_____
_____

Sources & Resources I'm Grateful For Today (Higher Power, Pets, Places, Things):
_____
_____
_____

Saturday _____
Date

Experiences I'm Grateful For Today (Events, Opportunities, Moments, & Sensations):
_____
_____
_____

People I'm Grateful For Today (Interactions, Conversations, Kindnesses Given or Received):
_____
_____
_____

Actions & Accomplishments I'm Grateful For Today (Big & Small):
_____
_____
_____

Sources & Resources I'm Grateful For Today (Higher Power, Pets, Places, Things):
_____
_____
_____

My Gratitude Year in Review

You've had an amazing year filled with documenting your gratitude! *In each area of your life, which experiences, people, achievements, and resources highlight your year?* Flip through the pages of this book and allow yourself to reexperience the grateful feelings.

Relationships	
Career	
Financial	
Living Environment	
Community Engagement	
Physical Health	
Mental & Emotional Health	
Intellectual Growth	
Recreation & Relaxation	
Spirituality	

ENDNOTES

[1] Emmons, R. (2010, November 16). Why gratitude is good. *Greater Good Magazine: Science-Based Insights for Meaningful Life*. Retrieved from: http://greatergood.berkeley.edu/article/item/why_gratitude_is_good

[2] Seligman, M. E. P., Steen, T. A., Park, N. P., & Peterson, C. (2005). Positive psychology progress: Empirical validation of interventions. *American Psychologist, 60*(5), 410-421. http://dx.doi.org/10.1037/0003-066X.60.5.410

[3] Gordon, C. L., Arnette, R. A. M., & Smith, R. E. (2011). Have you thanked your spouse today?: Felt and expressed gratitude among married couples. *Personality & Individual Differences, 50*(3), 339-343. http://dx.doi.org/10.1016/j.paid.2010.10.012

[4] Froh, J. J., Bono, G., Fan, J., Emmons, R. A., Henderson, K., Harris, C., . . . Wood, A. M. (2014). Nice thinking! An educational intervention that teaches children to think gratefully. *School Psychology Review, 43*(2), 132-152. Retrieved from https://www.researchgate.net/publication/273061748_Nice_Thinking_An_Educational_Intervention_That_Teaches_Children_to_Think_Gratefully

[5] Bartlett, M. & Arpin, S. (2019). Gratitude and loneliness: Enhancing health and well-being in older adults. *Research on Aging, 41*(8), 772-793. https://doi.org/10.1177/0164027519845354

[6] Krejtz, I., Nezlek, J. B., Michnicka, A., Holas, P., & Rusanowska, M. (2016). Counting one's blessings can reduce the impact of daily stress. *Journal of Happiness Studies: An Interdisciplinary Forum on Subjective Well-Being, 17*(1), 25–39. https://doi.org/10.1007/s10902-014-9578-4

[7] Digdon, N., & Koble, A. (2011). Effects of constructive worry, imagery distraction, and gratitude interventions on sleep quality: A pilot trial. *Applied Psychology: Health and Well-Being, 3*(2), 193–206. https://doi.org/10.1111/j.1758-0854.2011.01049.x

[8] Kashdan, T., Uswatte, G., & Julian, T. (2006). Gratitude and hedonic and eudaimonic well-being in Vietnam War veterans. Behaviour Research and Therapy, 44(2), 177-99. https://doi.org/10.1016/j.brat.2005.01.005

[9] Heckendorf, H., Lehr, D., Ebert, D. D., & Freund, H. (2019). Efficacy of an internet and app-based gratitude intervention in reducing repetitive negative thinking and mechanisms of change in the intervention's effect on anxiety and depression: Results from a randomized controlled trial. *Behaviour Research and Therapy, 119*, 1-12. https://doi.org/10.1016/j.brat.2019.103415

[10] Kaplan, S., Bradley-Geist, J., Ahmad, A., Anderson, A., Hargrove, A., Lindsey, A. (2013). A test of two positive psychology interventions to increase employee well-being. *Journal of Business and Psychology, 29*, 367-380. https://doi.org/10.1007/s10869-013-9319-4

[11] Kyeong, Sunghyon & Kim, Joohan & Kim, Dae & Kim, Hesun & Kim, Jae-Jin. (2017). Effects of gratitude meditation on neural network functional connectivity and brain-heart coupling. *Scientific Reports, 7*(1), 1-15. https://doi.org/10.1038/s41598-017-05520-9

[12] DeWall, C. N., Lambert, N. M., Pond, R. S., Jr., Kashdan, T. B., & Fincham, F. D. (2012). A grateful heart is a nonviolent heart: Cross-sectional, experience sampling, longitudinal, and experimental evidence. *Social Psychological and Personality Science, 3*(2), 232–240. https://doi.org/10.1177/1948550611416675

[13] Froh, J. J., Sefick, W. J., & Emmons, R. A. (2008). Counting blessings in early adolescents: An experimental study of gratitude and subjective well-being. *Journal of School Psychology, 46*(2), 213-33. https://doi.org/10.1016/j.jsp.2007.03.005

[14] Hill, P. L., Allemand, M., & Roberts, B. W. (2013). Examining the pathways between gratitude and self-rated physical health across adulthood. *Personality and Individual Differences, 54*(1), 92–96. https://doi.org/10.1016/j.paid.2012.08.011

[15] Chaplin, L. N., John, D. R., Rindfleisch, A., & Froh, J. J. (2019). The impact of gratitude on adolescent materialism and generosity. *Journal of Positive Psychology, 14*(4), 502-511. https://doi.org/10.1080/17439760.2018.1497688

[16] Petrocchi, C. (2016). The impact of gratitude on depression and anxiety: the mediating role of criticizing, attacking, and reassuring the self. *Self and Identity, 15*(2), 191–205. https://doi.org/10.1080/15298868.2015.1095794

[17] Lin, C. (2015). Self-esteem mediates the relationship between dispositional gratitude and well-being. *Personality and Individual Differences, 85*, 145-148. https://doi.org/10.1016/j.paid.2015.04.045

[18] Froh, J.J., Emmons, R.A., Card, N.A., Bono, G. & Wilson, J.A. (2011). Gratitude and the reduced costs of materialism in adolescents. *Journal of Happiness Studies, 12*, 289–302. https://doi.org/10.1007/s10902-010-9195-9

[19] Jackowska, M., Brown, J., Ronaldson, A., & Steptoe, A. (2016). The impact of a brief gratitude intervention on subjective well-being, biology and sleep. *Journal of Health Psychology, 21*(10), 2207–2217. https://doi.org/10.1177/1359105315572455

[20] Chaplin, L. N., John, D. R., Rindfleisch, A., & Froh, J. J. (2019). The impact of gratitude on adolescent materialism and generosity. *Journal of Positive Psychology, 14*(4), 502-511. https://doi.org/10.1080/17439760.2018.1497688

[21] Emmons, R. A., & McCullough, M. E. (2003). Counting blessings versus burdens: An experimental investigation of gratitude and subjective well-being in daily life. *Journal of Personality and Social Psychology, 84*(2), 377–389. https://doi.org/10.1037/0022-3514.84.2.377

[22] Killen, A., & Macaskill, A. (2015). Using a gratitude intervention to enhance well-being in older adults. *Journal of Happiness Studies: An Interdisciplinary Forum on Subjective Well-Being, 16*(4), 947–964. https://doi.org/10.1007/s10902-014-9542-3

[23] Kaplan, J. (2012). *Gratitude Survey*. John Templeton Foundation. Retrieved from: http://greatergood.berkeley.edu/article/item/how_grateful_are_americans.

[24] Emmons, R. A., & McCullough, M. E. (2003). Counting blessings versus burdens: An experimental investigation of gratitude and subjective well-being in daily life. *Journal of Personality and Social Psychology, 84*(2), 377–389. https://doi.org/10.1037/0022-3514.84.2.377

[25] Michie, S. (2009). Pride and gratitude: How positive emotions influence the prosocial behaviors of organizational leaders. *Journal of Leadership and Organizational Studies, 15*, 393–404. https://doi.org/10.1177/1548051809333338

[26] Wong, Y. J., Owen, J., Gabana, N. T., Brown, J. W., McInnis, S., Toth, P., & Gilman, L. (2018). Does gratitude writing improve the mental health of psychotherapy clients? Evidence from a randomized controlled trial. *Psychotherapy Research: Journal of the Society for Psychotherapy Research, 28*(2), 192–202. https://doi.org/10.1080/10503307.2016.1169332

[27] Burke, R. J., Ng, E. S. W., & Fiksenbaum, L. (2009). Virtues, work satisfactions and psychological well-being among nurses. *International Journal of Workplace Health Management, 2*(3), 202-219. https://doi.org/10.1108/17538350910993403

[28] Hoy, B., Suldo, S. M., & Raffaele Mendez, L. (2013). Links between parents' and children's levels of gratitude, life satisfaction, and hope. *Journal of Happiness Studies, 14* (4), 1343-1361. https://doi.org/10.1007/s10902-012-9386-7

[29] Howells, K. (2012). *Gratitude in education*. Rotterdam: Sense Publishers. https://doi.org/10.1007/978-94-6091-814-8

[30] Algoe, S.B., Gable, S.L., & Maisel, N.C. (2010). It's the little things: Everyday gratitude as a booster shot for romantic relationships. *Personal Relationships, 17*, 217-233. https://doi.org/10.1111/j.1475-6811.2010.01273.x

[31] Waters, L. (2012). Predicting Job Satisfaction: Contributions of individual gratitude and institutionalized gratitude. *Psychology, 3*, 1174-1176. https://doi.org/10.4236/psych.2012.312A173

[32] Froh, J. J., Kashdan, T. B., Ozimkowski, K. M., & Miller, N. (2009). Who benefits the most from a gratitude intervention in children and adolescents? Examining positive affect as a moderator. *The Journal of Positive Psychology, 4*, 408–422. https://doi.org/10.1080/17439760902992464

[33] Andersson, L., Giacalone, R., & Jurkierwicz, C. (2007). On the relationship of hope and gratitude to corporate social responsibility. *Journal of Business Ethics, 70*, 401–409. https://doi.org/10.1007/s10551-006-9118-1

[34] Froh, J.J., Emmons, R.A., Card, N.A., Bono, G. & Wilson, J.A. (2011). Gratitude and the reduced costs of materialism in adolescents. *Journal of Happiness Studies, 12*, 289–302. https://doi.org/10.1007/s10902-010-9195-9

[35] Wood, A. M., Joseph, S, & Linley, P. A. (2007). Coping style as a psychological resource of grateful people. *Journal of Social and Clinical Psychology, 26*, 1076-1093. https://doi.org/10.1521/jscp.2007.26.9.1076

[36] Vernon, L. L., Dillon, J. M., & Steiner, A. R. W. (2009). Proactive coping, gratitude, and posttraumatic stress disorder in college women. *Anxiety, Stress, & Coping, 22*, 117–127. https://doi.org/10.1080/10615800802203751

[37] Ruini, C., & Vescovelli, F. (2013). The role of gratitude in breast cancer: its relationships with post-traumatic growth, psychological well-being and distress. *Journal of Happiness Studies, 14*, 263-274. https://doi.org/10.1007/s10902-012-9330-x

[38] Ng, M., & Wong, W. (2012). The differential effects of gratitude and sleep on psychological distress in patients with chronic pain. *Journal of Health Psychology, 18*, 263-271. https://doi.org/10.1177/1359105312439733

[39] Lai, S. T., & O'Carroll, R. E. (2017). 'The Three Good Things'-the effects of gratitude practice on well-being: controlled trial. *Health Psychology Update, 26*, 10-18.

[40] Toepfer, S. M., Cichy, K., & Peters, P. (2012). Letters of gratitude: Further evidence for author benefits. *Journal of Happiness Studies: An Interdisciplinary Forum on Subjective Well-Being, 13(1)*, 187–201. https://doi.org/10.1007/s10902-011-9257-7

[41] Redwine, L. S., Henry, B. L., Pung, M. A., Wilson, K., Chinh, K., Knight, B., Jain, S., Rutledge, T., Greenberg, B., Maisel, A., & Mills, P. J. (2016). Pilot randomized study of a gratitude journaling intervention on heart rate variability and inflammatory biomarkers in patients with stage B heart failure. *Psychosomatic Medicine, 78(6)*, 667–676. https://doi.org/10.1097/PSY.0000000000000316

[42] Schnitker, S.A. & Richardson, K.L. (2019). Framing gratitude journaling as prayer amplifies its hedonic and eudaimonic well-being, but not health benefits. *The Journal of Positive Psychology, 14(4)*, 427-439. https://doi.org/10.1080/17439760.2018.1460690

[43] Southwell, S., & Gould, E. (2017). A randomised wait list-controlled pre–post–follow-up trial of a gratitude diary with a distressed sample. *The Journal of Positive Psychology, 12(6)*, 579–593. https://doi.org/10.1080/17439760.2016.1221127

[44] Wolfe, W. L., & Patterson, K. (2017). Comparison of a gratitude-based and cognitive restructuring intervention for body dissatisfaction and dysfunctional eating behavior in college women. *Eating Disorders: The Journal of Treatment & Prevention, 25(4)*, 330–344. https://doi.org/10.1080/10640266.2017.1279908

[45] Wood, A. M., Joseph, S., Lloyd, J., & Atkins, S. (2009). Gratitude influences sleep through the mechanism of pre-sleep cognitions. *Journal of Psychosomatic Research, 66(1)*, 43–48. https://doi.org/10.1016/j.jpsychores.2008.09.002

[46] Lambert, N.M., Clark, M.S., Durtschi, J., Fincham, F.D., & Graham, S.M. (2010). Benefits of expressing gratitude: expressing gratitude to a partner changes one's view of the relationship. *Psychological Science, 21(4)*, 574-80. https://doi.org/10.1177/0956797610364003

[47] Kini, P., Wong, J., McInnis, S., Gabana, N., & Brown, J. W. (2016). The effects of gratitude expression on neural activity. *NeuroImage, 128*, 1-10. https://doi.org/10.1016/j.neuroimage.2015.12.040

[48] Rash, J. A., Matsuba, M. K., & Prkachin, K. M. (2011). Gratitude and well-being: Who benefits the most from a gratitude intervention? *Applied Psychology: Health and Well-Being, 3(3)*, 350–369. https://doi.org/10.1111/j.1758-0854.2011.01058.x

[49] Kardaş, F., Çam, Z., Eşkisu, M., & Gelibolu, S. (2019). Gratitude, hope, optimism and life satisfaction as predictors of psychological well-being. *Eurasian Journal of Educational Research, 19*, 81-100. https://doi.org/10.14689/ejer.2019.82.5

[50] Salvador-Ferrer, C. (2017). The relationship between gratitude and life satisfaction in a sample of Spanish university students: The moderation role of gender. *Anales de Psicología, 33(1)*, 114–119. https://doi.org/10.6018/analesps.32.3.226671

[51] vanOyen Witvliet, C., Richie, F. J., Root Luna, L. M., & Van Tongeren, D. R. (2018). Gratitude predicts hope and happiness: A two-study assessment of traits and states. *The Journal of Positive Psychology, 14(3)*, 271–282. https://doi.org/10.1080/17439760.2018.1424924

[52] Wilson, J. T. (2016). Brightening the mind: The impact of practicing gratitude on focus and resilience in learning. *Journal of the Scholarship of Teaching and Learning, 16(4)*, 1–13. https://doi.org/10.14434/josotl.v16i4.19998

[53] Kloos, N., Austin, J., van't Klooster, J. W., Drossaert, C., & Bohlmeijer, E. (2022). Appreciating the Good Things in Life During the Covid-19 Pandemic: A Randomized Controlled Trial and Evaluation of a Gratitude App. *Journal of happiness studies, 23(8)*, 1001–1025. https://doi.org/10.1007/s10902-022-00586-3

About the Author

With over 20 years of expertise helping people transform their lives and careers, Dr. Colleen Georges is a life and career coach, TEDx speaker, founder of RESCRIPT Your Story LLC, and author of the 8-time award winning book, *RESCRIPT the Story You're Telling Yourself: The Eight Practices to Quiet Your Inner Antagonist, Amplify Your Inner Advocate, & Author a Limitless Life*.

Dr. Colleen's own experiences dealing with and overcoming anxiety, procrastination, perfectionism, and panic attacks have shaped her work helping others. In her TEDx Talk, *Re-Scripting the Stories We Tell Ourselves*, Dr. Colleen illustrates how we can achieve our goals and change our lives by RESCRIPTing the way we talk to and about ourselves. Through RESCRIPT Your Story LLC, she provides individual life and career coaching, leads community wellness groups, and delivers organizational trainings and speaking engagements. Dr. Colleen is also a Rutgers University Lecturer in counseling, women's leadership, and social justice.

She received her Bachelor's Degree in Psychology, Master's Degree in Counseling Psychology, and Doctorate in Counseling Psychology from Rutgers University. Dr. Colleen is a NJ Licensed Professional Counselor, Certified Life & Career Coach, Certified Positive Psychology Coach, Certified Goal Success Coach, Certified Anxiety Specialist, and holds over a dozen certifications in coaching and counseling.

Dr. Colleen's expertise has been featured in various media including News12, RVNTV, Huffington Post, Thrive Global, Forbes, Live Happy, Mashable, The Job Network, Care.com, Aspire Magazine, Formidable Woman Magazine, and New Jersey Family Magazine. She lives in Piscataway, NJ with her husband, José, son, Joshua, and cat daughter, Kitty.

To connect with Dr. Colleen, visit: www.ColleenGeorges.com

RESCRIPT Daily Goal Getting & Productivity Planner

The **RESCRIPT Daily Goal Getting & Productivity Planner** includes 365+ days for you to set and get your goals and track your productivity. It offers strategies for you to decide what you want to accomplish in each area of your life and gives you tools to create productivity habits that get things done! In the RESCRIPT Daily Goal Getting & Productivity Planner, you'll discover: research revelations that illustrate the kinds of thoughts and actions that foster goal success; how speaking to yourself with affirmations and defining your motivations cultivates positive action; how making time each day for experiences that bring you joy can foster happiness and productivity; how regularly noting your accomplishments and triumphs over challenges boosts confidence; and strategies for creating daily routines that start your day with motivation and end it with peace.

LET YOUR JOURNEY TO RESCRIPT & ENGAGE YOUR GOALS BEGIN!

www.RESCRIPTWorkbooks.com

RESCRIPT THE STORY YOU'RE TELLING YOURSELF:
THE EIGHT PRACTICES TO QUIET YOUR INNER ANTAGONIST, AMPLIFY YOUR INNER ADVOCATE, & AUTHOR A LIMITLESS LIFE

In the 8-time award-winning **RESCRIPT the Story You're Telling Yourself: The Eight Practices to Quiet Your Inner Antagonist, Amplify Your Inner Advocate, & Author a Limitless Life**, Dr. Colleen guides you on a self-authorship journey using the eight practices of her RESCRIPT framework, based in Positive Psychology. You'll discover how to identify limiting stories you're telling yourself that are keeping you stuck; quiet your Inner Antagonist quickly so it doesn't hinder you; amplify your Inner Advocate to cultivate positive thoughts and actions; stop criticizing yourself, dwelling on the past, and fearing the future; and recognize your self-worth so you can set and achieve your goals.

STOP THE NASTY CRITIC INSIDE YOUR HEAD FROM CONTROLLING & LIMITING YOUR LIFE

LET YOUR JOURNEY TO RESCRIPT BEGIN!

www.RESCRIPTBook.com

THANK YOU

My deepest gratitude to my family, friends, clients, students, and readers for always empowering and inspiring me to pursue my goals and passions. This journal could not have been created without you.

With Love,
Dr. Colleen

RESCRIPT THE STORY YOU'RE TELLING YOURSELF: THE EIGHT PRACTICES TO QUIET YOUR INNER ANTAGONIST, AMPLIFY YOUR INNER ADVOCATE, & AUTHOR A LIMITLESS LIFE

In the 8-time award-winning **RESCRIPT the Story You're Telling Yourself: The Eight Practices to Quiet Your Inner Antagonist, Amplify Your Inner Advocate, & Author a Limitless Life**, Dr. Colleen guides you on a self-authorship journey using the eight practices of her RESCRIPT framework, based in Positive Psychology. You'll discover how to identify limiting stories you're telling yourself that are keeping you stuck; quiet your Inner Antagonist quickly so it doesn't hinder you; amplify your Inner Advocate to cultivate positive thoughts and actions; stop criticizing yourself, dwelling on the past, and fearing the future; and recognize your self-worth so you can set and achieve your goals.

STOP THE NASTY CRITIC INSIDE YOUR HEAD FROM CONTROLLING & LIMITING YOUR LIFE

LET YOUR JOURNEY TO RESCRIPT BEGIN!

www.RESCRIPTBook.com

THANK YOU

My deepest gratitude to my family, friends, clients, students, and readers for always empowering and inspiring me to pursue my goals and passions. This journal could not have been created without you.

With Love,
Dr. Colleen

www.ingramcontent.com/pod-product-compliance
Lightning Source LLC
Chambersburg PA
CBHW081616100526
44590CB00021B/3457